Blessed Living

Blessed Living

The Gifts of the Beatitudes

C. DON JONES

WIPF & STOCK · Eugene, Oregon

Wipf & Stock
An Imprint of Wipf and Stock Publishers
199 W. 8th Ave., Suite 3
Eugene, OR 97401

www.wipfandstock.com

PAPERBACK ISBN: 979-8-3852-4599-4
HARDCOVER ISBN: 979-8-3852-4600-7
EBOOK ISBN: 979-8-3852-4601-4

VERSION NUMBER 07/09/25

For Kathryn

Oh my God, I think he's serious!

—FR. JOHN DEAR

Contents

Introduction

The Jesus Faith

THE LITTLE GIRL CAME back to the altar rail. Obviously, the bread and grape juice were a hit with this one. Her mother had lost hold of her hand and was now trying to get out from between the pews. The four-year-old was kneeling and smiling expectantly. The lay leader and I both smiled back.

"You can't have seconds," her mother said light-heartedly as she took her hand.

"Why not?" asked the lay leader.

Really! Why not? Does a child asking for more of "the snack" somehow shatter the feelings of reverence and sober reflection of Holy Communion? Yes, some serious stuff gets said by pastors as they recite the words of institution. "This my body given for you. This my blood poured out for you and for many for the forgiveness of sins." Thousands of years of debate have gone into the *meaning* of these words. But honestly, what could be more meaningful than the gratitude expressed by my own son when he was three years of age? He returned to his seat and said, "Tastes good, Mom."

What is the faith we talk about every Sunday? Is it Christianity, the family of God, the peaceable kingdom? The four-year-old girl previously mentioned usually addressed me as "Pastor Don" just like everyone else in her family did. There were occasions, though, when this honorific escaped her young mind. She would then get her point across by referring to me as "the church man" or more often "the Jesus man."

I like that.

What is this Jesus faith? We can define it as many people do. "We believe in Jesus Christ his only Son, our Lord." The Apostles' Creed appears to sum it up with that statement. Then there is the confession of the Ethiopian eunuch in the disputed text of Acts 8:37, "I believe Jesus Christ is the Son of God." Does a person have the Jesus faith by first believing certain doctrinal assertions about him? Surely someone *begins* having faith at some time. But what if the creedal formula has it upside down?

Jesus began attracting followers *before* any of them started calling him the Messiah or the Son of God. It was Jesus' own faith in God that brought his followers to their conclusions about him. The apostles declared him Messiah or Christ and the Son of God after they spent time with him and began listening to and traveling with him. Matthew quotes Jesus saying, "For flesh and blood did not reveal this to you but my Father in heaven" (16:17b). We are never told when that occurred. Presumably it was exposure to Jesus' life of faith—a combination of his life, teaching, and practices—that led them to their conclusions. Jesus' faith in the Father was different than anything in their experience. Jesus knows through his faith the Father is revealed to them.

When the young girl called me "the Jesus man," the association was not the same. She knew that I was connected to the place where her family went and people talked about Jesus. I was just the person doing the most talking when they were there. The real issue is whether Jesus ever gets to talk in those places of worship.

Let me share another story.

The Church of the Beatitudes sits on a mountain just above the site of ancient Capernaum by the Sea of Galilee. It is not an ancient structure. It was built in the twentieth century. The church has eight sides as well as an octagonal dome with eight stained glass windows. Each window has one of the Beatitudes from Matthew chapter 5 written on it in Latin. The church may not be on the top of the list for most people visiting Israel. It is very nice though. Among all the sites I was to see that day, it was the one I most wanted to visit.

There was a group ahead of us. We all have the experience when we are touring a zoo or a museum of someone either being ahead of us or behind us, adding unnecessary pressure to our visit. It can be very difficult to observe proper etiquette. Should I try moving forward? Perhaps I should try standing directly behind the people lingering over the exhibit to get the point across that other people are waiting. The group I was touring with was in the latter position behind another group that was not moving on and allowing us to proceed. The group ahead of us was a Korean Methodist choral group occupying the seats and they were . . . singing praises to God.

No one in our group really wanted to rush this choral group. It would just not feel right. Many of us felt we were somehow intruding and did not walk very far into the sanctuary. I, on the other hand, walked along the walls of the sanctuary during the singing. While I listened to the choir, I gazed at the windows above us. Standing along the walls gave me the angle I needed to read the words. Attempting to silently translate the Latin texts made my reading slower and more intentional.

"Happy are the poor in spirit. Happy are the meek. Happy are the pure in heart. Happy are the peacemakers. Happy are the persecuted. Happy are they who hunger and thirst for justice. Happy are they who mourn. Happy are the merciful."

I made the circle again reading the words a second time. Then I read them a third time. During this third reading, a realization came to me. It may have been the effect of what was happening. I did not know the language used by the choir and barely understood the Latin in which the words of Jesus were preserved. I was still participating in worship. The final book of the New Testament—the Revelation of Saint John—takes place during a time of worship. During worship, God's Spirit opens us to truths we often missed before or were not ready to know. In such times of enlightening, there can be only one response—prayer. Once the choir finished their song and filed out of the church, I went to one of the pews near the altar in the middle of the sanctuary and there prayed, "Lord, this is what you want me to know." I had been looking at everything from the wrong direction.

Do we have it backward? Are we thinking about faith and salvation the wrong way? Is a sincere desire to be obedient more important than assenting to theological truths? Perhaps a sense of gratitude is the most important element of salvation. I am inclined to think that wonder, appreciation, and imagination are important for spiritual development. These qualities lead people to the knowledge *of* God instead of knowledge *about* God. We must have the knowledge of something to speak about it. God is not an object in the relationship of what Martin Buber called I-It. God is only related to as I-Thou. The creed is good as any outline is good. Yet, we only have an I-It relationship to the words on paper. It is the same relationship as "keeping commandments."

The Beatitudes are expressions of the Jesus faith within the relationship of I-Thou. It is easy to fall into thinking of commandments as objects (I-It) in and of themselves. Think about how people like to wear "Ten Commandments" lapel pins or place signs on their lawns or courthouses. It is objectifying—something the people claim is holy and potentially absolute. The Beatitudes do not lend themselves to objectification as easily. They may be memorized and be treated as objects that way. Yet, faithful observance requires us to keep the commandments as the minimum and live beyond them in the Beatitudes.

The question of obedience to commands begins the process of defining the command. This is also the process of looking for loopholes. Consider the questions that arise when a Bible study group asks about the sixth commandment—"You shall not murder." It is true that the translation of the word for murder is in dispute, but that is not the issue. What is murder?

Is murder defined as killing another human being? Or is it the killing of an *innocent* human being? Christian leaders struggle with this distinction. What about killing in declared and justified wars? Is anyone truly innocent? These questions plague Bible group leaders. Historically speaking, it was not such a difficult question. All killing of human beings was deemed wrong for the early Christians. The participation of a Christian in warfare was discouraged if not condemned. Was not Jesus executed by an unjust imperial state? Who among his followers could then collaborate with the empire against other people?

The Christian West since World War II has struggled with this commandment. Fighting against fascism, Nazism, and imperialism is an act of justice. Church leaders were forced to take a longer look at the commandment after Hiroshima and Nagasaki. The carpet bombing of German cities meant that either all the people of Germany were guilty of Nazi crimes or that innocent human beings were made to suffer and die. Were our pacifist ancient forebears and our Anabaptist brothers and sisters correct all along? What would the world be like if the Allies had not fought their enemies? Did we see ourselves as heroes or as lesser evils? We have not yet shaken off this crisis of conscience.

We are not settling the argument here. If the plain statement of a command can be debated, how easily can the meaning of "Blessed are the poor in spirit" be debated? For the purposes of this study, we will compare the texts from Matthew and Luke to help us understand the writers' intentions and hopefully the intent of Jesus.

Translators use either the words "happiness" or "blessed" to give us the meaning of "beatitude." Most English translations begin each Beatitude with the words "Blessed are you . . . ." These words signify growth in spiritual maturity and happiness. The first Psalm pronounces beatitude on faithful people growing toward spiritual health. We begin by not taking the advice of wicked people.

> Happy are those who do not follow the advice of the wicked,
> or take the path that sinners tread, or sit in the seat of scoffers;
> but their delight is in the law of the LORD,
> and on his law, they meditate day and night. (Ps 1:1–2)

Happiness means we are either in or growing into the state of Godlikeness. Of course, that last word needs to be explained. Christians know we are creatures. Our state of being is the original created state of blessedness. This state of being is hidden in our experiences with other people. We actively hide it and sometimes deny it.

Jesus brings us to happiness as our liberator/redeemer and Lord. Christ exposes the image of God in us that we have hidden by sins. Jesus as Lord plants something new within us and makes it grow. It is the image of God in Christ. This is the miracle of the Holy Spirit. We are being made perfect in the love of Christ. Being remade in this perfection is more than simply acting as Jesus would. We eventually move beyond teaching and acting to becoming the image of Christ as St. Paul says, "All of us . . . are being transformed in the same image from one degree of glory to another for this comes from the Lord, the Spirit" (2 Cor 3:18).

What is the Jesus faith? Simply stated, it is Christianity that has grown and changed and changed again over two thousand years. The early disciples would not recognize modern Christianity as being their own until they looked more closely.

Jesus lived within the Israelite religion that first came from the stories of the exodus. Moses would not have recognized the practices of Jesus' day either, but he would know it when he heard the retelling of the stories and commandments.

Retelling is our goal here.

I

The Kingdom for the Poor and the Meek

Blessed are the poor in spirit, for theirs is the kingdom of heaven.
(Matt 5:3)

Blessed are you who are poor, for yours is the kingdom of God.
(Luke 6:20b)

IT WAS MY FIRST Sunday morning at a new church. When I met Andy, the sound system volunteer, he was dressed in a nice suit and wore a copy of the Ten Commandments on his lapel. I told him, "I will see your Ten Commandments and raise you Eight Beatitudes." He was taken aback for a moment, but I had made my first friend in that church. He got it, in other words. Months later, at that same church, I encountered a visitor who had not been to any church since he became an adult. When I mentioned the Beatitudes in a class setting, the visitor asked, "What are those?" Andy turned his Bible to Matthew 5 to help him read them. Unfortunately, this was not the last time it happened. Church people are more familiar with the Ten Commandments than the Beatitudes. Just as in Exodus and Deuteronomy we have two different versions of the Ten Commandments, so in the Gospels of Matthew and Luke there are two different versions of the Beatitudes. Yet, many Christian believers who do not attend church have never heard of the Beatitudes. It is a shame, and it is damaging to the faith.

The first question many people ask when looking at the first Beatitude in both Matthew and Luke is, "Did Matthew soften the Beatitude in some way?" I do not think so. In fact, Matthew appears to be extending the sense of this Beatitude. Jesus, like many preachers, may have proclaimed one version in one place and a different version in the other. If so, then these variants have the same meaning. The poor are blessed because the kingdom belongs to them.

There are those people who like to get bogged down in questions about the poor. Who is truly needy? Who among the poor deserves our help? Are we giving a hand up or a handout? Such questions are designed to allow for wiggle room. There are those who do not ever want to help people. A church member once claimed the policy of the local food bank was unfair because he could not receive free food, only poor people could. It is a bizarre claim. Because there are people who take such attitudes or want ceaseless debate, it seems good to place the Beatitudes blessing the poor with the one blessing the meek. There is some overlap between the two anyway.

What is poverty? It is more than not having enough to satisfy the necessities of life. A recent study from the *Journal of the American Medical Association* shows that deaths due to poverty in the United States are higher than gun violence or overdose.[1] Poverty is soul-crushing. Being poor provides limited access to educational opportunities and any financial security. The poor usually reside in harsh environments and circumstances with little access to healthy food. Being poor also means low wage employment while being caught in a cycle of living that both requires and punishes you for living beyond your means. An example of this problem is payday lending with punishing interest rates.

Over my years in ministry, I learned there is nothing quite as expensive as living in poverty. If you must live in a house that is not energy efficient, you spend more money heating your home. If you have a small medical issue, you wait until it is a major problem before you seek treatment. Transportation is often unreliable

1. Brady and Zheng, "Mortality Associated with Poverty," 618–19.

and, therefore, costly. Risks are taken in choosing to fulfill an immediate need such as food or rent and ignoring less urgent needs like healthcare, important vehicle maintenance, and paying taxes. Perhaps the worst risk taken by those living in poverty is the risk of rejection. Imagine needing to ask for help, asking for help, and then being told you are not worthy of help. Now suppose that rejection comes from a church that equates righteousness with being wealthy while separating the poor into two categories—the deserving and undeserving.

Modern economic doctrines claim to eliminate poverty. When they do not live up to the promise, blame is placed on the poor. The doctrine is never considered to be flawed by those who do not experience poverty. When I have tried teaching this Beatitude, there are often people who push back. The following dialogue is drawn from several like it.

"What is Jesus saying here?" I ask during a discussion of Luke's version.

"He means the poor in spirit," a wealthier older man in the congregation says.

"Let's look down to verse twenty-four," I begin. "But woe to you who are rich, for you have received your consolation."

"Okay."

"Is it possible he means woe to those who are rich in spirit?"

The last question is a conversation stopper. Jesus is talking about people who are in poverty in contrast to people who have an inordinate amount of wealth. Still, many class members are not convinced. The phone rings on Monday morning. The person on the other end takes issue with my assertion that Jesus is talking about poor people.

"He cannot be talking about those lazy, shiftless, addicts who won't work. The Bible says, 'If any won't work neither should he eat.'"

"Context," I think but do not say it out loud.

Prejudice runs as rampant in church as it does in society. Who is the lazy shiftless addict the church member is talking about? Does he know anyone in particular? Is he describing a relative he resents? If he cannot put a name to the person he describes, then it is an assumption about people he does not know. This is pre-judging or prejudice. Let's examine the context of the scripture people often cite in response to this Beatitude

"For even when we were with you, we gave you this com-mand: Anyone unwilling to work should not eat. For we hear that some of you are living in idleness, mere busybodies, not doing any work. Now such persons we command and exhort in the Lord Je-sus to do their work quietly and earn their own living. Brothers and sisters do not be weary doing what is right" (2 Thess 3:10–13). The context of this passage indicates that some members of the community were attempting to subvert the tradition Paul and oth-ers taught. They should stop causing trouble and work quietly and earn their own living. Paul and others did not accept the support of the congregations even though they had a right to expect it. The example they set reinforced the tradition they gave. Whoever the "busybodies" were, their effort was not helping build up the com-munity. They were not useful to the kingdom of heaven.

Jesus counted the poor among his followers. He reached out to impoverished people and stood up for them. He praised the widow who gave a pittance. Jesus warned that ignoring the im-poverished was a way of ignoring him. And he warned that riches were detrimental to salvation. The story of the rich young ruler is about a man who leaves Jesus and is sorrowful and unblessed because of his wealth. All he was required to do was let go of his wealth and give to the poor.

SERVING WEALTH

Jesus taught, "No one can serve two masters; for a slave will either hate the one and love the other, or be devoted to one and despise the other. You cannot serve God and wealth" (Matt 6:24).

Poverty can be spiritual as well as physical. The rich young ruler likely held a view that equates wealth with spiritual success. It was a common assumption that a few wealthy, righteous people really understood the ways of God. "But this crowd—that does not know the law—is accursed" (John 7:49). The assumption that righteousness brings material wealth is dangerous to the church. We run the risk of rejecting Jesus when he arrives as the poor.

Worshiping wealth is not discussed enough in the churches. One reason is that we have a difficult time doing ministries without money for facilities, equipment, and personnel. Another reason is there is always someone who does not wish to let go of any money and claims thrift is the Lord's true way. It is this desire for and worship of wealth that is the problem. "For the love of money is the root of all kinds of evil, and in their eagerness to be rich some have wandered from the faith and pierced themselves with many pains" (1 Tim 6:10). A volunteer approached the leaders of the congregation for money so the youth group could take a trip. A wealthy person on the board volunteered to pay the money out of his own pocket. He went on to say that when he gives money to a church project it is less meaningful than those who give their time. He reasoned that while not everyone has the same amount of disposable income, everyone has twenty-four hours in the day. His response came after the volunteer expressed gratitude for the monetary gift. The brief lecture from the wealthy man seemed unnecessary. Was his money a problem for his conscience?

The unfortunate truth is not everyone has the same amount of time within the day. Being a pastor and a parent, I was able to arrange my schedule for field trips and other school activities that many parents are unable to attend. There was some sense of privilege of time in my life. If a teacher thanked me for giving my time, it was just the same position as the wealthy person being thanked for a donation of cash. Such privilege places us in positions where it is easy to be proud in the worst sense.

The claim made in 1 Timothy about how people pursuing wealth pierce themselves with many pains is easy to understand in this light. What are we willing to sacrifice for the pursuit of wealth? Are we giving up health, time, and relationships? Are we willing to give up on God? Jesus discusses this while explaining the parable of the sower to the disciples. "As for what was sown among thorns, this is the one who hears the word, but the cares of the world and the lure of wealth choke the word and it yields nothing" (Matt 13:22). A family who decided to pursue wealth in the guise of getting out of debt illustrated this interpretation well. When we asked why they apparently dropped out of church, they replied they worked overtime on Sundays to pay for their cars, their home, and other possessions. They were also paying for new purchases bought but not on credit. Getting out of debt was a new way of worshiping wealth. They were pursuing their consolation—having material items, including a nest egg.

POVERTY AND DISCIPLESHIP

The phrase "poor in spirit" was used only once by the Qumran community made famous by the Dead Sea Scrolls. To them, the phrase meant the people of God: the people who are the "righteous remnant" awaiting their vindication in God's restoration of all things. So, what does that mean for us?

The imagery of a righteous remnant is found in both the prophets Isaiah and Jeremiah. The context of the famous virgin birth quote used by Matthew is in a dialogue the prophet Isaiah has with King Ahaz (Isa 7:14). The prophet brings his son Shear-jasub with him. The name means "a remnant will return." Ahaz is facing a war against the northern kingdom, Israel, and its northern neighbor, Syria. Ahaz could make an alliance with the Assyrian Empire. Isaiah warns him such a lopsided alliance is dangerous to the nation and the house of David. Ahaz does not listen to his advice. "I am your servant and your son," he says to Tiglath-Pileser of Assyria, "Come up, and rescue me from the hand of the king of Aram and the king of Israel" (2 Kgs 16:7b). He strips the temple to send gifts (tribute) to his new ally. Clearly the savior for Ahaz is the king of the Assyrians. Isaiah argued this savior will be a devastator. But a remnant will survive. Jeremiah tells us how the remnant survives.

Empires do not last forever. One replaces another eventually. Babylon replaced Assyria and consumed the southern kingdom of Judah. Jeremiah, like Isaiah, contended with kings and false prophets who convinced themselves they would be saved from the Babylonians. Once the people went into exile, they were given false hope of an immediate return.

> Thus says the LORD of hosts, the God of Israel, to all the exiles whom I have sent into exile from Babylon: Build houses and live in them; plant gardens and eat what they produce. Take wives and have sons and daughters; take wives for your sons and give your daughters in marriage, that they may bear sons and daughters; multiply there, do not decrease. But seek the welfare of the city where I have sent you into exile, and pray for the LORD on its behalf, for in its welfare you will find your welfare . . . . For thus says the LORD: Only when Babylon's seventy years are completed will I visit you and I will fulfill to you my promise and bring you back to this place (Jer 29:4–9)

The letter Jeremiah sent to the exiles helped preserve a remnant that would one day return to the holy city. His advice to the exiles is good for disciples who are poor in spirit. Hebrews embraces the theme of exile to give instruction. The remnant is not only a group of Israelites. They are faithful Israelites. They are righteous and just in their ways. So, again, what does this mean for us?

It means embracing simplicity, which is a goal easier talked about than accomplished. We live in a world of complex systems. I know someone who bought a freezer to fill it up with meat. I wondered out loud why anyone would believe if the food system collapsed electricity would be available. Embracing simplicity requires us to understand how things work. The COVID-19 pandemic introduced the phrase "supply chain" to non-specialists. One does not have to look very far to see how easily these systems of distribution break down. When it comes to money, few people really understand what it is. They simply know they need it to pay bills, buy groceries, clothes, gasoline, etc. To live comfortably, people require a lot of money. When prices rise, more money is required. There never seems to be enough money. The pandemic raised the question of what happens if one has the money but there is nothing to purchase. How are our needs to be met? Do we confuse needs with wants? When do our wants become our greed?

Simplicity—poverty for the Spirit—is the way that we conduct Christian behavior toward other people. The letters of Paul, including the ones that may not have been from his own hand, are filled with this sort of advice. "But we urge you, beloved, to do so more and more, to aspire to live quietly, to mind your own affairs, and to work with your own hands, as we directed you, so that you may behave properly toward outsiders and be dependent on no one" (1 Thess 4:10b–12). Another example is "Thieves must give up stealing; rather let them labor and work honestly with their hands, so as to have something to share with the needy" (Eph 4:28). In modern terms, these passages and others indicate the disciples of Jesus are meant to embrace simplicity to identify with and relate to the needy.

Disciples do not embrace poverty for its own sake. As we understand the spiritually crushing effects of poverty, it is a structural social evil. In the same way, disciples may embrace marginalized people but not marginalization. Jesus instructed would-be followers to give up their security to enhance the lives of the insecure.

The parables of the rich farmer (Luke 12:16–21) and the rich man and Lazarus (Luke 16:19–31) illustrate the woe Jesus pronounces on the wealthy in contrast to the Beatitude "Blessed are the poor." The rich men in the stories received their consolation. The reader of these stories should notice that on each occasion the rich person is consumed with themselves and their perceived needs. The farmer who builds larger barns and fills them plans to have a happy retirement. But he does not enjoy any more time on this earth. What was the point of all his effort? We do not hear about the brothers of the character in the second story until the end, and then only after *nothing* else is done for him, including his request that Lazarus be sent to relieve his thirst. This self-absorption is opposite to the nature of the poor in spirit.

The poor in spirit—the righteous remnant—are not self-focused people. Yet, it is a temptation to be self-absorbed even in poverty. The disciple of Jesus does not embrace poverty itself for this reason. The focus is on living a life that glorifies God. The focus is on neither the self nor the community. That mistake may have been made at Qumran where a separatist commune for holiness looked forward to the destruction of everyone else. Such an attitude is antithetical to the spirit of the Beatitudes taught by Jesus. The poor in spirit are those who embrace the poor by their own simple lives.

> Blessed are the meek, for they shall inherit the earth.
> (Matt 5:5)

The third Beatitude of Jesus appears to be a quote from Ps 37:11, "But the meek shall inherit the land, and delight themselves in abundant prosperity." The Greek translation of the Hebrew *anawim* translated above as meek is *prais*, which is used in the Beatitude. The words can also mean "poor." Is Jesus simply reinforcing the first Beatitude with this third one? I believe there is room in interpretation for that. It is likely that he has more in mind.

"Now the man Moses was very humble, more so than anyone else on earth" (Num 12:3). Miriam and Aaron are jealous of Moses. They attack his claim as prophet because they do not like his wife. God hears both their complaint and their claim to be prophetic leaders. Moses has the greater claim because he speaks to God "face to face" and sees the form of God. Yet he does not assert this claim. God testifies to it. Aaron, since he was the high priest, does not suffer any punishment. Miriam, however, is given a leprous skin disease and is banned from the camp for a week.

The verb form of the Hebrew word *anawim* also used for meek is used here to describe Moses. Being meek, poor in spirit, or humble is a value that is reinforced in the Beatitudes and throughout the New Testament. It is prized in the Hebrew scriptures as well, but it is subject to a great deal of debate in churches and societies. Is being meek a fulfilling way of life? What about the importance of having adequate resources? What about being left out of the good things of this life?

The difference between these questions and the intent of this Beatitude is apparent. Humility is not valued in our world. Heroes, in popular entertainment, are not humble. Yet, real heroes always are. An upperclassman in my high school was recognized as a football all-American lineman. In the spring, he was also on the track and field team with me. When I asked him to autograph my school annual, he wrote, "To a fun guy who honored me by asking me to sign his yearbook." He accomplished something greater, though, when he suffered a career-ending injury while playing for the University of Tennessee. He met the disappointment and coped with it better than many young men would have.

Would his apparent humility seem special if he had not been a star football player? He could have been arrogant, but he was not. He always stood up for other people, especially those who were bullied by other students. No one could mistake his meekness for being weak.

Saint Benedict speaks of twelve levels of humility in his *Rule* for monasteries. The chapter on humility is placed after the one dealing with restraint of speech. Humility is not a state of being. It is a spiritual practice. "God opposed the proud but gives grace to the humble." James quotes Prov 3:34 before continuing his admonition that ends with "Humble yourselves before the Lord, and he will exalt you" (Jas 4:10). James also gives this advice after warnings about how we speak to and about other people.

James and the writers of Proverbs understand humility is a product of wisdom. James sums up our difference between seeking self-fulfillment and being meek. "For where there is envy and selfish ambition, there will also be disorder and wickedness of every kind. But the wisdom from above is first pure, then peaceable, gentle, willing to yield, full of mercy and good fruits, without a trace of partiality or hypocrisy" (Jas 3:16–17). A wise person lives with these spiritual values. A person who will cause strife and turmoil will not value these attributes. Their wisdom is of the world. True wisdom is about thought and action. More importantly though, wisdom is about what we say. The voice we use to speak to other people and to God demonstrates the origin of our wisdom. The inner voice we use in speaking to ourselves does, too. We often fail to recognize these truths because of a lack of humility.

People who claim they can do nothing right, correctly, or properly often want someone to tell them differently. Who would not want to hear, "You're being too hard on yourself"? And who would not want the reassurance, "No one expects you to be perfect"? But Jesus calls for his disciples to be perfect just as the Father is perfect (Matt 5:48). Is he exaggerating to make a point of how our righteousness is meant to *exceed* that of the Pharisees? The scribes of the Pharisees taught the people that separation from evil and striving for holiness are based in keeping the *Torah*. Honestly, there is nothing wrong with that. The early disciples of Jesus admitted the goal of such perfection was impossible to achieve.

Pride is the opposite of humility. The New Testament uses many different words we translate as pride. The word "pride" has more than one sense in English in our day. There is a proper sense of taking pride in goodness. U2's song most people think is titled "In the Name of Love" is titled "Pride (In the Name of Love)." The other more negative sense is the opposite of humility. The English word "hubris" may be a more accurate translation. This idea of overconfidence or overestimating one's ability is what is being discussed in most instances in the New Testament. A humble person who does not know what to do will ask for help. Blowhards believe without any evidence that they know what to do. Hubris makes a person foolish. True wisdom, according to St. James, St. Paul, and St. Benedict, arises from a meek attitude.

When we speak of perfection, we do not really know what we are talking about. This hubris is the reason we fail. God wants no images of the divine self. We often think it is because we do not want to make the mistake of confusing the object we make with the one who makes us. Yet there is more to this commandment. God cannot be contained in temples, houses, or heads; however, this is not the reason why worshipers cannot have images to focus worship. The reason is surprisingly simple to miss. God is humble.

The Hebrew Bible is clear on many ideas about a warrior god, a storm god, and a jealous god. It is also clear that God is patient. But humble? Yes. Consider this: the temple of Solomon was nothing compared to the grandeur of the Great Pyramids or the Parthenon. The temple of Herod the Great was not one of the seven wonders of the world. There is nothing that indicates the Holy One of Israel wanted any of these monuments. It is strange for us to think about divine humility or meekness. Divine strength stems from divine humility.

Practicing meekness enhances our ability to be compassionate toward other people. Mutual love is only possible when the members of a community practice humility. Pride, boastfulness, and dominance are marks of weakness. Weak people threaten. People lacking courage try to hide it with bravado. These personalities do not do well within the community. Unfortunately, such people often get others to believe in abilities they do not have, nonexistent strength, and to take bravado seriously.

People who claim they have "the answer" are often the problem. This truth is the premise of Jesus' statement later in the Sermon on the Mount regarding false prophets (Matt 7:15–20). They are trees that bear bad fruit and are ravenous wolves disguised as sheep. Such people do not see themselves clearly either. The destructive personality type always has an answer or blame for someone else's issues. Jesus talks about this problematic busybody a few verses prior to the one about false prophets. "You hypocrite, take the log out of your own eye, and then you will clearly see to take the speck out of your neighbor's eye" (Matt 7:5).

False teachers and hypocrites do not practice meekness. They are not humble, nor they do represent God in any sense. In their pride, they are unteachable. Whatever spiritual gifts are possessed by these people are corrupted. "On that day many will say to me, 'Lord, Lord, did we not prophesy in your name, and cast out demons in your name?' Then I will declare to them, 'I never knew you; go away from me you evildoers'" (Matt 7:22–23).

How can we practice humility? Again, we return to Paul's advice "to aspire to live quietly, to mind your own affairs, and to work with your own hands, as we directed you, so that you may behave properly toward outsiders and be dependent on no one." We should add to that more advice in a later letter. "Do nothing from selfish ambition or conceit, but in humility regard others as better than yourselves. Let each of you look not to your own interests, but to the interests of others. Let the same mind be in you that was in Christ Jesus" (Phil 2:3–5). Later in the same letter he says the believers should be known for their gentleness (Phil 4:5).

Can a person learn to be humble alone? Moses was not always "the meekest man in all the earth." Readers that know his story know he first thought to free the Israelites by killing their Egyptian overseers. The Israelites saw no reason to trade one brutal overseer for another. He fled to the wilderness. During the next forty years, he learned the trade that was abhorrent to the Egyptians. Moses learned to herd sheep. He worked for his father-in-law while living as "a stranger in a strange land."

Humility is not easy to learn. For many of us, it is not part of our socialization. There is apparently no advantage to be gained in the world by practicing humility. Jesus knew this is how people behaved. He offered how to gain honor by practicing humility. "When you are invited by someone to a wedding banquet, do not sit down at the place of honor . . . go and sit down at the lowest place so that when your host comes, he may say to you, 'Friend, move up higher'; then you will be honored in the presence of all who sit at the table with you" (Luke 14:8–10). This strategy for gaining honor could easily backfire. The host may allow the person who takes the lowest seat to stay there. Anyone who becomes jealous or envious of someone else's honor does not have an attitude of humility.

St. Benedict allowed for his monastery to welcome priests into their membership. The priest would enter the novitiate and be seated at the lowest place among the monks. The only way to move to higher seating was when one of the brothers died. The only way to no longer be in the lowest place is for another new novice to enter the monastery. The sons of the nobles sat below the sons of the craftsmen. It was a tenure system based on how long a brother served in the monastic community.[2]

Pride, though, finds its way into each of us. A monk could presumably take pride in his tenure. Eventually, the monks took

---

2. See *Rule of St. Benedict*, chapters 58, 59, 60.

pride in being monastics, and late medieval monasteries often had hired servants to tend to the daily labor. Spiritual renewal in these communities all came from rediscovering the importance of humility in their lives together.

Moses learned humility in the field watching the sheep the same way his ancestor Jacob learned it. The work was not what he was educated to do. It may have been tedious and boring at times. But there had to be times that broke the tedium with excitement and danger. Predators could attack the flock. A change in the weather could threaten their health. Fire could be a danger if it got out of control. A burning bush would get a shepherd's attention.

Moses returns to Egypt with his family. Decades earlier he may have intended to return with an army. Now the shepherd carries no weapon. He carries the staff of the shepherd to lead the exodus of his people and bring them to the promised land.

Moses does not get to be in the promised land because his humility failed when he needed to show it the most. The people lacked water once again. They blamed Moses for taking them out of Egypt in the first place. Moses and Aaron had just buried their sister Miriam. It was getting difficult to have patience with the congregation in the wilderness. When Moses took the problem to God he was told to take his staff with him, assemble the people, and command water from the rock before their eyes. "So Moses took the staff from before the LORD, as he commanded him. Moses and Aaron gathered the assembly together before the rock, and he said to them, 'Listen you rebels, shall we bring water for you out of this rock?' Then Moses lifted up his hand and struck the rock twice with his staff; water came out abundantly, and the congregation and their livestock drank" (Num 20:9–11). Moses had his say and probably got everyone's attention with his violent display. But Moses made it look like he and Aaron through their own power brought water from the rock. God claims they did not treat God as holy before the eyes of the people. An early Christian preacher knew the frustrations a person could have with other people, including leading them. "For even as weeds are never lacking in a field, provokers are never lacking in the world. Therefore, that person is truly gentle who, when he or she has been offended, neither does evil nor even thinks of doing it."[3] God gave Moses a way to fill the need of the people without being contentious. Moses, feeling the bite of the criticism leveled at him, decided instead that he and his brother needed vindication. In fact, he did vindicate himself. What did it cost him? He led the people to the promised land. He did not lead them into it.

EARTH: LAND OR WORLD?

What exactly do the meek inherit? Moses led the Israelites out of slavery to the land of promise. They were Abraham's heirs. The divine promise made to him was passed to them. They were delighted in the fertility of the land. Water was abundant when compared to Egypt. Families could thrive there. A new life was set before them.

The image of the meek inheriting the earth is different than Israel entering the promised land. The psalmist claimed the meek will inherit the land and receive prosperity. But it is not what Jesus appears to be saying in Matt 5:5. As mentioned earlier, it is argued by some scholars that this Beatitude is merely a restatement of the first one. The meek are the "poor in spirit." Inheriting the earth is the same as receiving the kingdom of heaven. This is a means of spiritualizing the intent of the Beatitude. In this interpretation, the meek will inherit the new heaven and earth. Jesus, however, taught that humility is practiced in this world with results in this world that point to a future vindication from God.

The meek and humble are often not valued in this life for their ways. Ecclesiastes tells of a wise person delivering a city and being soon forgotten (Eccl 9:13–16). The meek may be valued when their contributions are understood later. The contributions of the meek are often unrecognized because they do not make a show of their efforts. Someone else must see it and make it known. Mother Teresa would not have been so well-known if journalist Malcolm

---

3. Quoted from an anonymously written, incomplete homily on Matthew shared in Simonetti et al., *Ancient Christian Commentary on Scriptures*, 83.

Muggeridge had not produced the documentary *Something Beautiful for God*. She would not have proposed a documentary about herself. In an age of advertising, press releases, and selfies, self-promotion is understood for what it is even though, to many people, it is distasteful. Respect that is worthwhile is given to those who do not seek such popularity. The work that continues to be fruitful over time does not rely solely on the presence of the person who builds their reputation on it. One detrimental effect of the spotlight on Mother Teresa was the assumption of many that *she* was the work. She was adamant that she was not. Another question should be asked now.

Are the meek better suited to solving most of our social problems? If we think about the fact that organizing neighborhoods requires knowledge of what should be done with a willingness to step back while other people do their tasks within the organization, then the meek are the best suited. During my ministry, I have served two churches with community gardens in two different towns. One was organized by a person who asked for help in making the garden. The other was organized by someone who scolded and cajoled people into using it. I often asked why some of the produce of the latter was not taken to a local food bank. The answer was "they can come get it themselves." A lot of the produce went uneaten because of that attitude.

A food desert can be made better when neighbors pitch in and help. The community can become more cohesive as neighbors work together. Ultimately, it is better than doing something *for* another person. Preserving the dignity of a person in a vulnerable position is a practice of humility.

Herman Jent, a dentist who was also a lay preacher, was annually sent by the local health department to examine the teeth of the "indigent children" of the school district. He chose to keep the students from feeling singled out because of their poverty. He asked the teachers to send a child whose parents he knew to come with the student designated by the health department. He did this to preserve the dignity of the children and their parents. Once when a little girl exclaimed the daddy of the student he was treating was in jail. He turned and told her she was not invited to bring that information. She was there to help the other students not to be frightened. If the student sitting in the room knew the dentist, it made him less of a stranger. I reflect on this example because he lived and practiced in a time when children were not allowed to question what adults, especially medical professionals, did. Few adults questioned the actions and conclusions of such professionals then too. He chose the humble way of Jesus to help the oral health of children. One could say Herman practiced and then preached it.

Humility allows the helpers to see those they wish to help as human beings of equal worth. When we see another person this way, we act in ways to preserve their dignity. If we embrace the poor, we accept being embraced by them.

"You are the salt of the earth," says Jesus a few verses later in Matt 5. What does that mean? First, the word "earth" is the same as the Beatitude. Salt has many uses. It can flavor and preserve food. It is necessary for health. Likewise, salt is used to increase the fertility of the earth. Too much of it destroys health and makes the land unusable. Jesus does not describe this though. He asks what happens when the salt loses its effectiveness. It is worthless. In modern usage, the phrase "salt of the earth" describes people who are honest, are hardworking, and mind their own business.

The properties of salt give it the ability to hold water in the soil. When we consider the results of corporate farming where the soil is depleted while waterways are poisoned, food is produced for a cheap price, but a great cost. On the other hand, we have more intensive farming methods that keep the soil fertile and protect the health of the waterways from erosion. The food produced in this way is often better tasting and healthier. Unfortunately, this type of food often sells for a higher price. What do the farmers have the next year in both instances? What do they inherit? Which method requires an attitude of meekness or humility?

The meek will inherit the *earth*—this planet, this land. The important actions of preservation and making the land more fertile are going to be done by people who consider the importance of others before they consider themselves. And they are the ones who can be trusted to do the same with a new earth and heaven.

2

Solace for the Mourners

Blessed are those who mourn, for they will be comforted.
(Matt 5:4)

Blessed are you who weep now for you will laugh (Luke 6:21b)

KING SAUL WAS LIKE a son to Samuel. The prophet recognized Saul, like himself, was chosen by God for a hard and perhaps thankless task. He anointed Saul as king of Israel. Samuel always had mixed emotions about doing this. He was brought to God's service as a child. Samuel was called into the place of his foster father, Eli. And his own sons, like Eli's, were not worthy of succeeding him. Saul was his successor. In fact, he was replacing Samuel in the prophet's own lifetime.

The struggle with bringing Saul into his role as king was not as difficult as bringing him into the role of God's servant. Saul never understood the two roles went together. The problem with Saul was he was always most concerned about his status before the people. His obedience to God was always of secondary importance.

Saul worshiped the God of Israel and no other. He made sacrifices to God, but his sacrifices were not acceptable. On one occasion, "Samuel said, 'What have you done?' Saul replied, 'When I saw the people were slipping away from me, and that you did not come within the days appointed, and that the Philistines were mustering in Michmash . . . so I forced myself and offered the burnt offering" (1 Sam 13:11–12). Samuel tells Saul that his royal line will not continue beyond him. Saul did not learn his lesson.

Samuel mourned for Saul after another occasion of disobedience. Saul was to fight and destroy the Amalekites and all their property. After the battle, he set up a monument to himself and kept Agag the king as captive and everything of value.

> When Samuel came to Saul, Saul said to him, "May you be blessed by the LORD; I have carried out the command of the LORD." But Samuel said, "What then is this bleating of sheep in my ears, and the lowing of cattle that I hear?" Saul said, "They have brought them from the Amalekites; for the people spared the best of the sheep and the cattle, to sacrifice to the LORD your God; but the rest we have utterly destroyed." (1 Sam 15:13–15)

Samuel decides it is time for Saul to stop talking. He has a message from the God that he must deliver. Samuel spent the night living through several emotions. At first, he was angry that Saul had once again disobeyed. Then, in anxiety, he cried out to God all night. He mourned with the same sorrow that God claimed for making Saul king. He also mourned for the lost son he had in Saul.

King Saul protested to Samuel he had obeyed and brought sacrifices for God. Samuel then gives a prophecy that became a theme for Israel's prophets. "Has the LORD as great delight in burnt offerings and in sacrifices, as in obedience to the voice of the LORD? Surely, to obey is better than sacrifice, and to heed than the fat of rams. For rebellion is no less a sin than divination, and stubbornness is like iniquity and idolatry. Because you have rejected the word of the LORD, he has also rejected you from being king" (1 Sam 15:22–23).

Jeremiah is known as "the weeping prophet" because, like Samuel was to Saul, he was to the king and all the people in Jerusalem. The people trusted in their might, their walls, and their preferred beliefs that the Babylonians would be defeated. Their religion was very important to them, too. They believed nothing could harm the people who gathered around "the temple of the LORD." Somehow, like King Saul, they believed that God's favor was found in the things they preferred doing. God was, in their minds, bound to do what they believed was good for them. They did not understand the impact of this sinful attitude on the community.

No action taken by the people of Jerusalem was worse than reversing the Jubilee. The people, along with King Zedekiah, freed all their Judean slaves. They made a covenant before God in front of the temple of the LORD. "But then you turned around and profaned my name when each of you took back your male and female slaves . . . . Therefore, thus says the LORD: You have not obeyed me by granting a release to your neighbors and friends" (Jer 34:16–17a).

Why would the people do such a thing? It appears to have been an action taken falsely out of desperation. The Babylonian army was rampaging through Judah. Zedekiah was facing judgment for treachery. So, he commanded that the slaves be liberated. They were free until the danger passed. Then the king allowed the freed people to be enslaved again. Jeremiah prophesied the Babylonian army would return and destroy the people for their blasphemous behavior. The king would not be spared.

Jeremiah mourned for the city before and after it was destroyed. The temple where the LORD's name was foresworn (taken in vain, you might say) over the slaves was destroyed along with the city. Yet Jeremiah remained with the people who were left by the Babylonians, warning them to finally obey what their God was telling them to do.

We can see how much love is grieved when the tragedy could be avoided. And yet, tragedy came. The people refused to see it. Jeremiah knew he could not force the people to understand and repent. He mourned being helpless to stop it.

Personal sins also cause mourning. A person realizing their own sinful acts will mourn until forgiven. We may lose the mournful nature of confession in liturgy sometimes because there is an anticipation of forgiveness being pronounced from the altar. "In the name of Jesus Christ, you are forgiven!" However, some sins are grieved over because they are hidden. As a friend says, "We are only as sick as our secrets."

Individual people and families will approach a clergy person who is not their own pastor to discuss something very troubling. Why would they not go to their own pastor? It could be their pastor does not keep confidences. More likely though, they want to appear a certain way to their pastor and will let their guard down to someone else. It is a sad commentary when pastors fail in confidential matters or practice judgmentalism. But it is a great example of how a personal sin can cause another person to continue to mourn without hearing a word of grace from the clergy. Church people play terrible games to keep up appearances and fail one another.

Genesis is filled with examples of personal sin causing grief in the lives of other people. Abel's murder left Adam and Eve bereaved of both sons. Rebekah feared Esau would kill Jacob and thereby lose both her sons. Jacob's older sons sell Joseph, the favored son, into slavery. Potiphar's wife levels a false accusation against Joseph, causing his imprisonment. And the chief cupbearer to Pharaoh forgets his promise and leaves Joseph in the prison. Personal sin causes disruption and grief to others. Sometimes, the only action we can take is to mourn.

SUFFERING FROM SIN

The story of the man born blind presents a bad assumption about sin and suffering. The apostles ask Jesus if the man was blinded by the sins of his parents or his own. Jesus says sin is not the reason the man is blind. God's glory is revealed in his healing. Bad things do not only happen to bad people. John tells us how the man later suffers from the sin of his parents. When asked if this was indeed their son, if he had really been blind from birth, and how it is he now has sight, they reply, "We know this is our son, and that he was born blind; but we do not know how it is that he now sees, nor do we know who opened his eyes. Ask him; he is of age. He will speak for himself" (John 9:20–21). They abandon their son out of fear, John tells us, because the leaders would turn anyone confessing Jesus out of the synagogue. They feared losing their place in the community. At the end of the story all the man has left is the Son of Man who healed his vision. We are reminded of Ps 27:10, "If my father and mother forsake me, the Lord will take me up."

The followers of John the Baptist questioned Jesus and his disciples about fasting. Why do Jesus and his followers not keep regular fasts like John's followers? Regular fasting is a practice intended to take our minds off self and our own strength to consider how God fills our needs. It is not a matter of self-reliance or willpower. Fasting is intended to help us understand our need for grace in the world and is accompanied with grief. We feel in fasting the suffering of other people who do not have our own security in food or other necessities in life. John's followers are right to be concerned. "And Jesus said to them, 'The wedding guests cannot mourn as long as the bridegroom is with them, can they? The days will come when the bridegroom is taken away and then they will fast'" (Matt 9:15).

Weddings are celebrations. People expect to feast, sing, dance, and indulge in high spirits. Weddings that are canceled at the last minute, or when one of the two getting married does not show up, are confusing and difficult. No one knows what the response of the guests should be. Some weddings are canceled due to tragedy. The promised future cannot happen. Families and guests mourn deeply. The loss at the time makes the tragic circumstances much worse. Jesus' followers will fast soon enough.

The examples above are difficult situations that just happen from time to time. When they happen, no one knows what to do. There is also suffering that is unavoidable. If it was not for the sin of other people, the suffering would not happen. When we look back to the story of the rich man and Lazarus, we see both types at work.

Lazarus means "leper." He is "covered with sores." Jesus is not telling a story about a man named Lazarus. He is speaking of a man who gets called Lazarus. He suffers because of an illness. But his suffering is made worse because lepers were set apart and could not participate in the community. They were simply considered dead while they still breathed.

The suffering of Lazarus is due to sickness, and it is made worse by a common attitude toward people with his disease. But the rich man participates in the suffering of the leper at his gate. Lazarus is allowed to starve to death by a person who could give him some relief. The structural sin of society and the personal sinful attitude makes the sick man's life worse.

Systemic sin causes suffering and mourning among those who are harmed. These sins also infest the hearts and minds of those who benefit from them. "Then Jesus said to his disciples, 'Truly I tell you, it will be hard for a rich person to enter the kingdom of heaven. Again, I tell you, it is easier for a camel to go through the eye of a needle than for someone to enter the kingdom of God'" (Matt 19:23–24). That familiar couplet is illustrated in the story of the rich man and Lazarus. The sin is so deep in the heart of the rich man that he requests Lazarus leave paradise to serve him a drop of water in torments. He would cause the suffering of someone else for his comfort. That is who he is and was in the story.

The Beatitude includes a promise. Those who mourn will be comforted. Those who weep now will laugh. The promise is redemption for them.

COMFORT AND LAUGHTER

Jesus gives a promise that is expressed in two ways. Those who mourn will be comforted. You who now weep will laugh. There are some awful things that happen to people that we are helpless to stop. Let's also think about the power of being forgiven for what we *stop* doing.

Some months ago, I gave a sermon on prayer. In the congregation sat a couple who had been members at a mega-church in the Chicago area. During my sermon they realized that they could not remember a time the big mega-church ever had prayer during worship times. Likely, they encouraged personal prayer. But they never had a "confession and pardon" or the Lord's Prayer. They never prayed together as the church. They were an audience and not a congregation. They had an enjoyable time in "worship," yet they missed the joy and comfort of a community.

The story of Ruth and Naomi is about two women mourning their losses. Naomi has lost her husband and sons. One of those sons was Ruth's husband. Naomi gives Ruth the opportunity to leave her and return to her birth family. Naomi is leaving the territory of Moab to her ancestral home in Judah. Ruth chooses to go with her. In doing so, Ruth knows she is choosing to live a life of mourning with Naomi. When she arrives home, Naomi renames herself *Marah* because of the bitterness in her life.

Ruth supports herself and her mother-in-law by menial labor. She becomes a gleaner. When wealthier people finished harvesting their fields, the common practice was any dropped grain could be retrieved and kept by the poor in the community. It was hard work. Women who gleaned were often subjected to suffering outrages by the men doing the heavier harvesting.

Ruth gleans one of the fields owned by Boaz, who respects what she has done for Naomi. Boaz orders his men to leave her alone and to drop a little extra grain for her. Ruth tells Naomi about all this man did for her. When Naomi hears his name, she declares Boaz is a "near kinsman" to her husband and sons. Maybe Ruth has stumbled onto their salvation? Boaz could potentially serve as the "kinsman-redeemer" for Ruth and Naomi to take over Naomi's property and to end the bitterness of their lives.

Job's life became bitter with similar losses to those of Ruth and Naomi. He laments how his friends and relatives abandoned him in his distress. However, in defiance to the accusations that evil results come from evil deeds, Job replies, "For I know that my redeemer lives, and that at the last he will stand upon the earth; and after my skin is destroyed, then in my flesh I shall see God, whom I shall see by my side, and my eyes shall behold and not another" (Job 19:25–27). Job seeks justification. He receives comfort and restitution in the end of the book. Ruth sees her redeemer in Boaz. God provides comfort and justification of her act of faithfulness to Naomi.

Redemption was practiced in many ways. A slave could be freed. An indebted person could have someone else pay the debts. A piece of land that had been sold could be bought back for the family. Ultimately, redemption was to happen in the years of Jubilee, which were supposed to be practiced every fifty years. Liberty came with restoration of status and lands.

A strong messianic image of this Jubilee is found in Isaiah. "The Spirit of the Lord GOD is upon me because the LORD has anointed me; he has sent me to bring good news to the oppressed, to bind up the brokenhearted, to proclaim liberty to the captives, and release to the prisoners; to proclaim the year of the LORD's favor" (Isa 61:1–2a). Luke uses this passage to demonstrate the beginning of Jesus' ministry and ultimate rejection (Luke 4:16–30).

Jesus claims, "Today this scripture has been fulfilled in your hearing." It strikes me that this is the beginning of an incomplete thought. Does he mean the fulfillment is in the reading? They do not see any miracles or deeds described in the text. They only hear it being read to them. Luke goes to the controversy that occurred while Jesus spoke. Luke tells his readers the fulfillment came by the person doing the reading. The disciples who heard this gospel read out loud knew they were not seeing the fulfillment. They were participating in it.

The examples Jesus gives are how grace came to people who were not Israelites in the times of Elijah and Elisha. They received the grace belonging to the people of God. Luke expects his listeners to know this about themselves. They are the people receiving the good news and liberty proclaimed by the prophets of old.

The Beatitude we consider here is when Jesus says, "Blessed are you who weep for you will laugh." Are laughter and comfort the same thing? Laughter can bring comfort. It can also inflict pain and cause others to weep. Isaac means laughter. Both Abraham and Sarah laughed at the words of God when they were told they would have a child. Sarah flipped the derisive laughter she experienced into laughter of the blessing of the child born to her. Ruth gives birth to Obed after her marriage with Boaz. But the child is considered Naomi's own. The women of the town tell her the son "shall be to you a restorer of life and a nourisher in your old age" (Ruth 4:15a). The child is a gift from the daughter-in-law who loves her.

Joy follows restoration. When loss is suffered and mourned, there is joy when the loss is restored. Joy is the theme of the searching shepherd, the woman who lost a coin, and the father with two sons in Luke 15. Joy and celebration come from such restoration. Joy and celebration also come when the blind receives sight, the poor are delivered, and liberty is proclaimed.

Laughter or comfort? Why not both? Those who mourn and weep need the comfort and joy of the liberty of the people of God.

When have we mourned, and it turned to comfort? When did we weep, and it turned to laughter? At the graveside service of their mother, my brother-in-law and his sister gave away packets of seeds. Their mother was an avid gardener. Kathryn likes sunflowers so I took some of those seeds and planted them in our flower bed. The neighbors asked about our beautiful sunflowers. We told them how we got them. Even in our mourning, we look for redemption or at least inspiration. Seeking redemption should be acknowledged when we have lost something or someone. We keep our feet moving. The result is not restoration to what was, but a restoration to what is greater. Job found such blessings on the other side of his turmoil. It is an ending that makes the story more palatable to us. One asks, though, if it was truly palatable for Job.

Was it necessary for Job to suffer due to a heavenly contest? It is wrong to interpret Job as an explanation of why we suffer. It only shows an explanation of why a person suffers is wrong. Job's friends believe a righteous person should not suffer loss. Job does, too. His friends all say he should confess the terrible sins he must have committed. Job claims he is innocent. However, if he had been in the place of a friend to someone suffering, Job would have argued that some unknown sin had taken hold of the person's life.

Job's children were gone. Yes, he was given more, but they could not replace the ones he lost in the storm. It is important to note that God answers Job from within a similar storm. Job lost his possessions and health, but he grieved for his children. Grieving parents are not satisfied with substitutes. People often say that parents are not supposed to bury their children. Yet throughout human history parents have buried many children. Something about it seems wrong to us. The psalmist who saw Jewish children killed by the Babylonians did not wish for their conquerors to die before they watched their children be destroyed (Ps 137).

A Russian-born Israeli poet, Abba Kovner, wrote a pamphlet in 1942 during the German occupation titled "Let Us Not Go as Lambs to the Slaughter." He failed to begin a Jewish uprising in Vilna. After the war, when the horrors of the Holocaust were first being revealed, Kovner and a group of other like-minded Jewish fighters formed a paramilitary organization called *Nakam*, which translates as revenge in English. They desired to kill as many Germans as there were Jews murdered during the war.[1] When does mourning turn to genocidal anger?

The Rwandan genocide in 1994 where members of the Hutu tribe murdered members of the Tutsi tribe left the world stunned. Western media used terms like "biblical proportions" to describe the numbers refugees and murder victims. The murders happened over ten weeks, making getting accurate numbers of victims difficult. The range estimated is between five hundred thousand and the official Rwandan estimate of one million. Another group of victims were ten thousand Twa people in the region. The Twa people lost about one-third of their population.[2]

Revenge killings in both cases were discouraged by leaders among the victim groups. Mourning turning to anger is understandable. Anger being turned back into mourning is how powerless people cope with the losses. Is this justice denied? Yes, it is. How do we keep this fact from destroying us?

A Dominican nun, the mother superior of a convent at Vilna, Anna Borkowska, helped Abba Kovner in the early days of the Nazi occupation. She told him she prayed for him and believed it was not enough. "What else do you need?" she asked. Kovner

1. Holocaust Encyclopedia, "Abba Kovner."

2. See McDoom, "Contested Counting"; and Sheshadri, "Pygmies in the Congo Basin."

asked for grenades. Somehow, she found three and despite her vows gave them to him. It was her convent that sheltered him and other young Jews from the Nazis. A couple of years later the convent was closed and Anna was arrested. She survived, and, forty years later, received the Righteous of the Nations award. Abba Kovner brought it to her from Israel. According to the Yad Vashem website, Anna Borkowska, then no longer a nun and eighty-four years old, asked why she deserved the medal. Abba Kovner replied, "You are Anna of the angels. During the days when angels hid their faces from us, this woman was Anna of the Angels. Not of angles we invent in our hearts, but of angels that create our lives forever."[3]

We can debate whether the gift of the grenades was right or wrong in this situation. The question she asked obligated her to do as requested. Yet, this was only part of the obligation she and the other sisters undertook for the sake of people they hoped to save from being murdered. She asked Kovner at one point to take her to the ghetto in Vilna. When he asked why, she said, "because God is there." Still, he refused. He felt the need to protect this non-Jewish woman whom he and the others with him called in Hebrew *Ima*, or mother. Did her example bring solace for the man who wanted more than anything genocidal revenge? She did help at least some. At the ceremony honoring her, Kovner still called her *Ima* though she was no longer a nun. She was an angel—a messenger from the God in which he no longer believed. Time does not heal all wounds, but love goes a long way toward it.

GIVING SOLACE TO MOURNERS

"It is better to go to the house of mourning than to go to the house of feasting; for this is the end of everyone and the living will lay it to heart .... The heart of the wise is in the house of mourning; but the heart of the fools is in the house of mirth" (Eccl 7:2–4). Many statements we use to provide "comfort" to people in mourning are more about our discomfort than that of the person in mourning.

3. Yad Vashem, "Borkowska, Anna."

If we tell grieving parents that God took their child "because he needed another angel," we are not helping the parents. Instead, we are trying to make ourselves feel better by saying something that sounds vaguely religious. God is made out to be a monster by such words. Another one we use, "they are now in a better place," shows that we would prefer to be somewhere other than with those who are mourning the lost loved one.

Jesus raises Lazarus and Jairus's dead daughter, which causes awe and rejoicing. We do not hear Jesus deny Mary by saying, "Lazarus is in a better place." Jairus does not hear, "She is one of God's little angels" either. People suffering or in mourning make the rest of us feel uncomfortable. We are, as Ecclesiastes says, to take it to heart even though we would prefer to avoid it.

I went to the funeral home to confer with the director about a funeral for a member of my congregation. The parking lot was empty except for a familiar van that I saw every month at the food bank. When I left the director's office I saw a woman from the family. Her look upon seeing me showed she recognized me.

"Have you lost someone?" I asked.

"Elmer," she said flatly. Then she added, "Mom's in the chapel."

I guessed she meant the old man who usually drove the van. I did not know his name until then. I always referred to him as "the General." He wore his hair and beard the length one sees in photographs of Civil War generals. The rebel flag license plate helped me think of the image, too.

I walked into the chapel while the family sat alone with Elmer lying in his open and very plain coffin. I went into professional mode as I spoke to the family and offered to pray with them. After the prayer, his widow asked, "Can we still get food from the food bank?" I had come from there and told her it was now closed for the day.

"Not today," she began. "We moved and don't know if we can come for food."

When she explained to me where they were now residing, I was certain it was outside of the area we served. I dropped out of professional mode. The answer was not going to be helpful in their mourning. The professional attitude was my way of avoiding the discomfort of the situation. Usually, my work with grieving families includes a lot of friends and relatives being there for support and providing meals for everyone. This situation was very different.

Elmer's family never said anything about when a funeral service would take place. The funeral home had nothing on the board about a receiving friends, funeral, or graveside service for this man and his family. Never once before had a family asked if they were going to be able to eat in the future.

I responded, "You will have to ask at the food bank office to be sure."

Apparently, this family was grieving more than the loss of the father and grandfather. They lost a home and a food resource. How do we provide solace? Saying the gentleman was in a better place would have implied they were left to fend for themselves—that God had made no provision for them. The discomfort I felt kept this memory with me. It is burned into my conscience.

Providing comfort for those who mourn is not easy. The early church recognized the process of grieving liturgically. The Eastern churches hold services for the departed on the third, ninth, and fortieth day after the death. They also mark the six-month and first anniversary of the death with special services. The Western practice of burial after the third day sometimes happens while the family is in a state of shock and not yet ready to grieve. Unfortunately, the community practices leading up to the funeral end, leaving the extended family to continue providing comfort.

Mourning comes in many forms. We may be grieving without acknowledging it ourselves. A grieving friend may snap at you when you offered to help. The action is wrong but understandable. The person needs understanding. Sometimes we are very thoughtless with our help too. It requires some reflection and consideration on our part. Reactions from mourners are normal.

We Bought a Zoo is a film about a family in grief. It is one of my favorites. It is loosely based on the book by Benjamin Mee. Having lost Katherine, who was their emotional rock, the family attempts to escape their grief by moving to a broken-down zoo to start a new life. The zoo, the animals, and the employees all suffer from some sort of loss in their lives. Spar, an aging tiger who is also the main attraction of the zoo, is at the end of his life. We learn through Benjamin's reluctance to develop an end-of-life plan how his response to grief is to fix problems. He intends to keep Spar alive despite everything he is told by the zookeeper and the state regulator. Benjamin wants to know how to make everything better for everyone. He believes if he fails, it will be just like Katherine's death.

The audience is never told how Katherine died. Benjamin tries to make his failure up to his children—Rosie and Dylan. As the story unfolds, he manages to make his zoo into a grieving *community* where each person works through their own grief in the project of reopening the zoo. The zoo and the family will continue in the future. The audience is left knowing the characters *have* a future. Early in the movie, everyone's grief is morbid. At the end of the film, most are working through their grief in healthy ways.[4]

Jesus brings healing in his ministry on earth. The apostles practiced healing as part of their ministries. They healed people from a variety of ailments as well as demonic possessions. Peter, upon healing a man at the gate of the temple, used the healing to illustrate the universal restoration that would come with Jesus' return (Acts 3:17–21). As discussed above, Jesus restoring dead loved ones to their families was a form of healing grief. This form of restoration included the healing of broken social relationships. Once healed lepers showed themselves to the priest, they were admitted back into the community. Before Jesus raised Jairus's daughter, an unnamed woman suffering an apparently continuous flow of blood receives healing power by touching Jesus. Instead of claiming she had stolen the power, Jesus commends her faith and declares her healed. She is no thief, and the problem that made her unclean to the rest of the community is no longer a problem.

Grieving people feel as though their loss places them outside the normal community life. They can feel either invisible or

4. Crowe, *We Bought a Zoo*.

too visible. Are mourners no longer what they once were? Is the loss somehow their new identity (widowed, divorced, childless, orphan)? It may help us if we ask ourselves what labels we give people. Our eyes may be opened to consider what expectations we put on some people.

My work as a pastor puts need and grief into focus many times. My grandmother died on a Saturday. The youth minister called me when he heard about it. "Don't worry. I have Sunday morning covered," he said. I could be with my family during our grief. But when my grandfather died it was different. The night he passed a beloved member of my congregation died, too. My family made the arrangements for my grandfather's funeral. The family of the lady from church made their arrangements for the same day as my grandfather's funeral. It was not easy, but I was present for both. I left the graveside of one and drove the two hours to be at my grandfather's funeral. I wore the same clothes to both funerals. It was a long day. The hardest part was not letting my grief turn to resentment at the other family or their dead loved one.

THE SOLACE OF LAST THINGS

Eschatology is the theologian's doctrine of final things. While many Christians focus on the dispensational doctrine of the "last days," eschatology is about the importance of the final actions taken by God for earth and its people. A familiar passage from the Revelation of St. John says, "See, the home of God is among mortals. He will dwell with them as their God; they will be his peoples, and God himself will be with them; he will wipe away every tear from their eyes, Death will be no more; mourning and crying and pain will be no more, for the first things have passed away" (21:3b–4). The first things are done. The time of universal restoration promised by Peter comes, and the final things—what we have all been praying for—are here.

The woe that is pronounced in Luke opposite to the Beatitude includes the eschatological hope of judgment upon evil. "Woe to you who are laughing now for you will mourn and weep" echoes the concern expressed by the psalmist when he complains, "For I was envious of the arrogant and saw the prosperity of the wicked .... They set their mouths against heaven, and their tongues range over the earth" (Ps 73:3).

We could demand from God some answers about people who cause the suffering of others. What ultimately happens to murderers we do not believe got the punishment they deserved? What about those who commit terrible crimes and are never caught or held accountable? We could tell ourselves we hunger and thirst for justice in these cases. However, we should consider the later words of the psalmist. "When my soul was embittered, when I was pricked in the heart, I was stupid and ignorant; I was like a brute beast toward you" (Ps 73:21–22). This is a person who rejoices in the suffering of other people. We could ask, "Well, are they not guilty?" Most assuredly they are, but why rejoice in their suffering? Now they mourn. Who will provide solace for them?

These questions muddy the waters of final things. Who has the wisdom to punish appropriately or decide to forgive? Both Matthew and Revelation declare God is among humanity. God is the only one fit to judge anyone else. Cruel and sadistic people who do not appear to have a conscience live among us too. God may remove them. Or God may purge their cruelty. The doctrine of final things shows us that ultimately God judges, decides, and saves. Our hope is that whatever happens God places us all into a state of being where our sins are no more. We no longer mourn over our own sins or the sinfulness of the world around us.

Is this "pie in the sky when you die" escapist theology? No. We now turn to Abraham and Sarah and the promises made to them. God makes two promises to Abraham that are never fulfilled in his lifetime. Nevertheless, they were fulfilled.

The first promise is that he and his heirs will have the land of the Canaanites. He never owned the land. Yet, he was able to live there as would any bedouin. He had no permanent city, house, or holding except for the tomb bought from the Hittites. The promise was always there with a partial fulfillment pointing toward the future.

The future though was difficult to fulfill without an heir, which was the second promise. Sarah offered to provide an heir for Abraham through her maid Hagar. Soon, though, Sarah realized she could not be satisfied with another woman providing an heir for her husband. Her attempt to overcome her and Abraham's mourning turned to mistreatment and resentment against an Egyptian slave.

The second promise was not only about one heir. Abraham was told his descendants would be as numerous as the stars. The heir that Sarah would bear would be the beginning of the many offspring promised. Sarah, though, was over such promises. Abraham laughed at God for promising the now apparently impossible. Yet, Sarah gave birth to Isaac because "God has brought laughter to me; everyone who hears will laugh with me" (Gen 21:6b).

The story of the Hebrew scriptures centers on fulfilling these promises. They are partially fulfilled in the lifetimes of Abraham and Sarah with the ultimate fulfillment going beyond their time. The three Abrahamic faiths all claim some part of that fulfillment. It is not difficult then for us to consider that mourning should be comforted now while expecting an ultimate solace later for all.

Jesus took lessons like the promises made and fulfilled to Abraham and Sarah for a better understanding of how solace or comfort should be there for everyone who mourns. As we have seen, he did what he could to alleviate the suffering that caused mourning among other people. It is telling that he never promised the healing for individuals would only come after they died. Neither does he see human suffering as necessarily redemptive. Some Christians believe personal suffering should be offered up as a sacrifice for the glory of God. Many times, the person suffering has no other option. Yet, those who teach this do not believe the suffering of others is to be ignored either. We are the partial fulfillment of comfort for suffering for many people. God is the ultimate fulfillment. When it comes to healing mourning for us or others, prayer for wisdom, insight, and ability is important to doing such work.

3

The Need for Righteousness
and the Grace of Mercy

Blessed are those who hunger and thirst for righteousness,
for they will be filled. (Matt 5:6)

Blessed are you who are hungry now for you will be filled. (Luke 6:21a)

WHAT DOES IT MEAN to be hungry and thirsty for righteousness? Is
it a deep desire to be a righteous or just person? Is it a deep desire
to see that righteousness and justice are upheld and practiced by
others? Is it both? But then, what does righteousness mean when
Luke is obviously talking about people being literally hungry, fam-
ished, or starving? These questions and others make agreeing on
and interpreting this passage difficult.

Being hungry and thirsty for righteousness has no meaning if
we do not understand actual hunger. Matthew makes this apparent
in the parable of the separation. "Then the king will say to those at
his right hand, 'Come, you that are blessed by my Father, inherit
the kingdom prepared for you from the foundation of the world;
for I was hungry and you gave me food, I was thirsty and you gave
me something to drink . . ." (Matt 25:34–35). In this parable, the
righteous are the ones who alleviated the suffering of Jesus by feeding the poor. Matthew ties the hope of the final restoration to acts

of righteousness and justice that will be ultimately fulfilled. The judgment described in the parable of the separation is when all the nations of the world will be brought before the Son of Man. The nations will be divided into two groups. One group practiced righteousness in the form of aid to people in need. The other group will be those who looked away when they saw people in need.

Is this what Matthew means in the Beatitude? What does the Son of Man say in the parable? "Come you that are blessed by my Father, inherit the Kingdom prepared for you from the foundation of the world." He pronounces the blessed happy state on those who inherit the kingdom.

Matthew talks about righteousness while Luke talks about hunger. Before we say more about hunger, let's discuss the meaning of righteousness. Most people, I think, avoid the word because everyone condemns self-righteousness. To avoid being seen that way we try to get away from a sense of real righteousness.

The structure of the Gospel of Matthew involves seven discussions of the meaning of righteousness. Jesus ends the parable by proclaiming those who inherit the kingdom "righteous." Matthew is indeed very interested in the subject of righteousness. The Greek word for righteousness, *dikiasune*, can also be translated as justice. It is sometimes difficult for translators to decide which translation is more accurate in a given context. When we look at this word in the context of the parable, it appears that justice is the proper term. When we consider the same word in the Beatitude, it is a little more difficult, and that opens up many alternative and parallel interpretations.

Let us consider two well-known passages concerning righteousness/justice in the Prophets. "He has told you, O mortal, what is good; and what does the LORD require of you but to do justice, and to love kindness, and to walk humbly with your God?" (Mic 6:8). "Look at the proud! Their spirit is not right in them, but the righteous live by their faith" (Hab 2:4).

Now consider the following passage. "The days are surely coming, says the LORD when I will raise up for David a righteous

Branch and he shall reign as king and deal wisely, and shall execute justice and righteousness in the land" (Jer 23:5).

The first text from Micah uses the word *mispat* for doing justice. The second one from Habakkuk uses the word *tsedeqa* for "the righteous who live by their faith." The final passage from Jeremiah speaks of the righteous (*tsedeq*) Branch who will do *mispat* and *tsedeqa*. What we learn from looking at these passages is the Hebrew prophets believed the righteous practiced justice. These two values are to be practiced by those who hunger and thirst for righteousness.

We really do not have one without the other. John Wesley talked about personal and social holiness. He was looking at the roots and fruit from the same tree. If we are truly righteous, we will do justice. If we attempt to do justice and are unrighteous personally, we may never know how we should do justice.

Hunger is real even in lands of plenty. The U.S. Department of Agriculture (USDA) labels certain people and entire communities as being "food insecure." A more commonly used term is "food deserts," which describes a type of food insecurity. Some urban communities do not have easy access to nutritious and fresh food. There is nowhere to go and buy food near where they live. Supermarket chains do not place their stores in these areas because they will not be able to make enough money. People living in these areas need transportation to other communities that are more profitable for the big supermarket chains.

Food banks and other forms of food outreach, such as community gardens, help alleviate the problem. These efforts do not, however, solve the problem. Pastors are often invited to serve on boards of directors for local food banks. One statistic during my time on one such board sticks with me. We were only serving 70 percent of the population the USDA labeled as food insecure in our area. But that same 70 percent was not able to receive enough food for a month from us. The clients used their EBT debit cards after they saw what we could give them. We were merely a supplement for their needs. We were not the solution.

The narrative of Ruth and Naomi shows how the work of gleaning was meant to help impoverished people (mainly women) receive food. But the actions Boaz takes indicates that gleaning was known not to provide enough food. Ruth practices righteousness in aiding her aged mother-in-law. Yet, despite the romanticism of the foreign woman supporting an Israelite widow, the struggle of many people in that time and ours is real. Why is food not made more available than it is? The question is always that of money.

Pastors in rural areas will watch in anger and despair as good vegetables rot in the fields. The vegetables are the leftovers after the processing companies have received their order. The contract the farmer received from the company stipulates that no more produce can be sold or even given away. This practice keeps rival processors away. Though there is no good reason people cannot be invited to the fields to get the fresh food they need, it is not allowed by the contract. Farmers post signs, close the access to the fields, and often poison what they can. No gleaning is possible given the relationship between farmers and processors.

It is hard to think Jesus would allow such actions to go unchallenged. After being criticized for allowing his disciples to glean on the Sabbath, "He said to them, 'Have you not read what David did when he and his companions were hungry? He entered the house of God and ate the bread of the Presence, which it was not lawful for him or his companions to eat, but only for the priests" (Matt 12:3). The bread of the Presence was only for the priests. However, the lives of starving people take precedence. Jesus says the Sabbath law forbidding work does not exist to keep hungry people from eating either. Interpreters may argue the motivation for the critics was simply to come up with any accusation. Perhaps this interpretation is correct, but our present time shows that some institutionally minded people do not care if people go hungry.

Fear of not having enough does not only affect the people who face hunger. It also motivates people who hoard food. During the pandemic, people panic-bought supplies and food. Families bought new freezers to store food they were hoarding as they feared the collapse of the food system. One person said, "Those people scare me more than the virus does." She had a point. Something goes wrong with the mindset of people consumed by fear. They believe there will not be enough, and by panic-buying, they ensure there will not be.

The Lord's Prayer is about having faith to forgive, to overcome temptation, to live the kingdom of God in this world, and to rely on divine provision (Matt 6:9–14). "Therefore, I tell you, do not worry about your life, what you will eat or what you will drink, or about your body what you will wear. Is not life more than food, and the body more than clothing? Look at the birds of the air; they neither sow nor reap nor gather into barns, and yet your heavenly Father feeds them. Are you not of more value than they?" (Matt 6:25–26).

Jesus tells his listeners there is more to life than worrying over our basic needs. Fulfilling our basic needs is not to change who we should be as his followers. Yes, food is important. But it is not the end all and be all of life. When we allow people to starve their hunger gets in the way of fulfilling their potential as human beings. Hungry people are not treated as though they were worthy as children of God. Needing to constantly beg to satisfy physical hunger keeps spiritual thirst and hunger from being satisfied.

SPIRITUAL HUNGER AND THIRST

Being hungry and thirsty for righteousness and justice includes more than working toward these goals. Christians are expected to satisfy our own spiritual hunger and thirst. Concerns over one's own physical needs and wants can be confused. The Israelites wandering in the wilderness complained they were bored with the bread from heaven and longed for the variety of food that some of them had in Egypt (Num 11:4–6). But the bread from heaven served more than one purpose. God "humbled you by letting you hunger, then by feeding you with manna, with which neither you nor your ancestors were acquainted, in order to make you understand that one does not live on bread alone, but by every word that comes from the mouth of the LORD" (Deut 8:3). The Israelites needed to know their physical wants were not the most important needs in their lives. This is the lesson Jesus declares during his own wandering in the wilderness.

Earlier generations of faithful people learned this lesson as well. According to the first line of Ps 63, it is "a Psalm of David, when he was on the wilderness of Judah." This is the same wilderness where Jesus fasted and prayed for forty days before beginning his ministry. The next lines begin the song. "O God, you are my God, I seek you, my soul thirsts for you; my flesh faints for you, as in a dry and weary land where there is no water" (Ps 63:1).

The writer speaks of David knowing his need to satisfy his thirst for God is as important as his need for water. This text may also refer to the time David and his men ate the bread of the Presence. We do not know. The fifth verse continues, "My soul is satisfied as with a rich feast, and my mouth praises you with joyful lips."

David was satisfied physically and spiritually. Praise was his response. He was truly filled.

FOR THEY WILL BE FILLED

Matthew also tells us about Joseph the righteous. As the betrothed husband of Mary, he decides to divorce Mary quietly rather than have a public spectacle. Matthew says he does this because he is a "just man" (Matt 1:19–23). He is a righteous man. What should he have done? One option he could have taken was to disgrace her and her family in a public way. He demonstrates his righteousness by not doing that. During a dream, an angel encourages him to finish the betrothal and raise the child who will be the Messiah. Joseph's desire for righteousness is being filled when his righteousness helps bring about the fulfillment of the hope of Israel.

The promise of fulfillment is in both versions of this Beatitude. This promise for citizens of the kingdom of God is the only one where there is a direct fulfillment of the spoken need. The poor in spirit are not promised riches. The peacemakers are not ensured peace, but hungry people will be filled physically and spiritually. The *Magnificat* of Mary includes the verse that God "has filled the hungry with good things" (Luke 1:53). Hungry people receive justice in the form of their need being fulfilled. Jesus added a woe to this Beatitude in Luke. "Woe to you who are full now for you will be hungry" (Luke 6:25a). This woe echoes Mary's later statement, "the rich are sent away empty."

The fifth book of the Psalms begins with thanksgiving for deliverance from turmoil. "For he satisfies the thirsty; and the hungry he fills with good things" (Ps 107:9).

The promise of fulfillment of both physical and spiritual hunger tests our trust. We should rely on God for our daily provision, and we should find ways to help other people receive their daily provisions. It is difficult to reconcile the two without an understanding of the interdependence of everything in God's world. We live on food. But we do not live on food alone. Our lives are not full without listening to and practicing divine justice.

The prophet Amos gave a warning in his day that the time would come upon the northern kingdom, Israel, when it would experience a famine not of bread but of hearing the prophetic words (Amos 8:11–14). People will despair in their hunger and thirst for these words. Why will this happen? Israel was very wealthy and pious, but they were very unjust to the poor. They sold bad food to them and defrauded them in many other ways.

The description of thirst and hunger points toward spiritual fulfillment. We live on food. We do not live on food alone. Most people going to church today are people who know they have a spiritual need, but we may not always know what that need is.

King David knew something was wrong. He had done wrong by both Bathsheba and her husband Uriah the Hittite. As time went by, he thought the matter was settled. Then he heard the words of the prophet and declared death for a man who stole a pet lamb. His unjust actions caused his self-righteousness and caused him to pronounce an unjust condemnation. Then the prophet said, "You are that man" (2 Sam 12:7a).

David's spiritual need could not be satisfied until he confessed his wrong. This need for confession is why those who hunger and thirst for righteousness and justice are blessed because their desire will be filled.

The problem with a promise in this Beatitude is the implication that not seeking after righteousness and justice will leave all of us in despair of ever seeing it happen. We may find ourselves claiming God has abandoned us, but we will feel abandoned because we abandoned the least of these.

> Blessed are the merciful, for they will receive mercy.
> (Matt 5:7)

The man was relieved. God had favored him in his anguish and worry. He was no longer in debt to the title company. Quietly, he expressed his thanks to God as he loudly thanked the loan manager. The tightness in his neck and shoulders gradually released as he walked to the parking garage.

The sun had come out from behind the cloud when he saw the familiar shape of someone—a man—Jim walking toward him. The other man abruptly stopped and turned the other direction. The man scoffed. Too late, he thought to himself, I already saw you.

"Jim!" he shouted.

The other man quickened his pace and kept walking.

Our man trotted after him. "Jim," he called again. "Don't run away from me."

Jim knew other people were watching by this time. He stopped, sighed, and turned to meet the man.

"Why did you run away?"

"Are you really going to make me say it? Fine. I don't have the money I owe you." Then he hastily added, "But I will get it to you as soon as I can."

The man nodded solemnly . . . and then he smiled. "No need to run away. I don't need the money anymore. Buy my lunch today, and we will call it even."

Jim did not know what to say. "Thank you," he began, "where do you want to go?"

Standing in front of his window the loan officer smiled. He, too, heard the man shout out to the other one and wondered what the shouting was about. He saw the relief in Jim's face and was satisfied he had done the right thing.

Jesus gives a parable where things did not turn out so well (Matt 18:23–35). The disciples heard from the conclusion that the story could have turned out differently. "So my heavenly Father will do to every one of you, if you do not forgive your brother or sister from your heart." How much better would it be for everyone in the story if forgiveness had continued? Yet, in the happier version given above, we do not know if the chain of mercy will continue. All we can know is that it should.

Shakespeare gave us the line "The quality of mercy is not strain'd." Mercy is not in any way constrained.[1] Portia, the character giving the speech, calls it an attribute of God. Portia is correct. Matthew makes about ten references to mercy throughout his book.

"Happy are those who are kind to the poor" (Prov 14–21b). This Beatitude comes from the Hebrew Bible. The ancient Greek translation known as the Septuagint (often designated by the Roman numeral LXX) translates into English as "happy are those who show mercy to the poor." The immediate context of the passage speaks to our tendency to treat the wealthy with deference while showing contempt for the poor. It is a rare occasion when we treat the rich the same way we treat the poor. James expresses this same thought when he cautions the church of his day about inviting the rich people who come to their assemblies to take places of honor while making the poor feel unwelcome. He says in doing this the early believers do not fulfill the "royal" law, "You shall love your neighbor as yourself." James concludes the section with "for judgment will be without mercy to anyone who has shown no mercy; mercy triumphs over judgment" (Jas 2:13). Many of us are familiar with the traditional version of the Lord's Prayer where we say, "forgive us our trespasses, as we forgive those who trespass against us." The version found in Luke reads, "And forgive us our sins for we ourselves forgive everyone indebted to us" (Luke 11:4b). In other words, as we forgive those who owe us money.

---

1. Shakespeare, *Merchant of Venice*, act 4, scene 1.

One may easily dismiss this Beatitude in either of two ways. The first is to assume because we have a generally good disposition to human beings, we do this as a matter of course. The second is to assume we should not fool ourselves into thinking it is ever possible to show mercy to everyone. Either way is deceptive.

What is mercy then? Mercy is how we treat people who do terrible things or fail in other ways. Mercy keeps peace between individual people, between and within communities, and between people and God.

Mercy is not easy to cultivate. People who were brought up being shown little mercy in their lives will find it difficult to follow an example they never had. There is also a fear that other people will take undue advantage of our mercy. The apostle Peter asked Jesus, "How many times shall I forgive my brother? As many as seven times?" The way Peter asks the question makes one assume he thought seven was an excessive number of times. Jesus replies, "Not seven times but seventy times seven" (Matt 18:21–22). English translators do not agree. Many modern translations give a varied number such as seventy-seven or four hundred ninety times. Most pastors and teachers agree Jesus places no limit to the number of times his followers should forgive.

Jesus continues with the parable mentioned above concerning a king who decides to settle accounts with his servants. One cannot repay his debt and begs for mercy. The king forgives the debt. The same servant, deciding never to be caught so short again, goes out with renewed boldness to force another servant to repay his debts to him. He does not accept his fellow servant's plea for patience and sends him to prison. When the king learns what happened he says, "You wicked servant! I forgave you all that debt because you pleaded with me. Should you not have had mercy on your fellow servant as I had mercy on you?" (Matt 18:32b–33).

It is said every human being has a blind spot. Our eyes are not perfect. In fact, there is a design flaw. The optic nerve that extends from the back of the brain attaches at the center of the eye. Our brains fill in the missing information, so we do not notice it. People also have moral blind spots. We believe we see the failures of others very clearly while we cannot see our own. The first servant who owes the king the larger debt does not see the same good he could have done for another servant. Often, we see the wrong done to us without seeing the good we may do instead.

The story of Cain's descendent Lamech gives us some insight here. After being wounded (or insulted), Lamech retaliated with murder. He brags to his wives, "If Cain is avenged sevenfold, truly Lamech seventy-sevenfold" (Gen 4:24). Nabal, in his story, refuses to supply David and his men. His wife Abigail placates David, so he does not kill Nabal, her, and all the family. When Nabal learns of his wife's action, he dies drunk and outraged (1 Sam 25:2–38). Both the names Lamech and Nabal can be translated as "fool" or "clown."

The moral blind spot is involved in both instances. David and his men have protected Nabal's family. Seen from David's point of view his request is reasonable. Nabal decides to ignore his previous benefit and returns an insult instead. Lamech is making a boast in the safety of his own home. But Peter is not interested in stories. He wants to know what is *required* of him. If grace comes with strings attached, is it really grace?

Grace and mercy work together. The difference between the two is grace is the free gift while mercy is the act of giving the gift. Jesus responds to his critics, "Go and learn what this means, 'I desire mercy and not sacrifice'" (Matt 9:13a). He does this more than once in Matthew. The phrase originates with the prophet Hosea, "For I desire steadfast love and not sacrifice/the knowledge of God rather than whole burnt offerings" (Hos 6:6). The word the NRSV translates as "steadfast love" has an ambiguous meaning. Possible translations include lovingkindness, mercy, and loyalty. These terms all fit together in some way.

Peter asked the wrong question. Do mercy and grace have limits? No. What then is humanly possible? That is a difficult question to answer. We could forgive seven times or four hundred ninety times many possible sins committed by another person, but there are some sins that appear unforgivable by those people who suffer because of them. Brutal crimes, such as rape or murder, are for most victims and their families too hard to forgive. Anyone counseling a victim of this kind of brutality to forgive their attacker expects peace without justice. The other words used to translate "steadfast love"—lovingkindness and loyalty—in Hosea bring justice and restoration into the discussion of forgiveness. What is restoration after brutality? Can the murdered child be brought back? Can a lifetime of abuse have no negative consequences for the abuser and the victim?

The principle of "a life for a life, and an eye for an eye" is about retaliatory justice when restoration is practically impossible. However, it is a form of justice that never heals because of the imbalance of power in the relationships of people. The law must intervene because of the imbalance of power among individuals. If the law says a life for a life, the power is in the law to retaliate or destroy.

"No mercy" is the tough person's declaration. Our society sees a lot of those instances where people intend to get revenge, have vengeance, or even the score with someone for injuries real or imagined. The braver person tries to find ways to show mercy and make peace.

Mercy is asked for. It is never demanded. As Shakespeare claims, mercy is an attribute of God. It is always a gift. Mercy is why peacemakers are called the children of God.

JUSTICE AND ONLY JUSTICE

"You must not distort justice; you must not show partiality; and you must not accept bribes, for a bribe blinds the eyes of the wise and subverts the cause of those who are in the right. Justice and only justice, you shall pursue, so that you may live and occupy the land that the LORD your God is giving you" (Deut 16:19–20). We are tempted, in light of this text as well as others, to consider justice as the highest standard for community life while mercy can only be extended by individuals. We owe this idea to Reinhold Niebuhr, who argued this point in his classic *Moral Man and Immoral Society*. What happens when a person is condemned by the courts but forgiven by their victim? Usually, the state's justice will continue to be administered.

The text from Deuteronomy quoted above is an unfortunate translation. *Tanakh*, the Jewish Bible distributed by the Jewish Publication Society, translates the last verse better: "Justice, justice, shall you pursue that you may thrive and occupy the land that the LORD your God is giving you." The sentiment that those who judicate should pursue justice and not bribes is the same. The idea they should only pursue justice is not the same. Justice is imperative, but justice alone does not give life.

Naim Ateek, a Palestinian priest in the Anglican Communion, says, "Aristotle defined justice as refraining from . . . gaining some advantage for oneself by seizing what belongs to another . . . or by denying a person that which is his or her due."[2] He later says regarding the connection of righteousness and justice, "Each dimension is important; each can be seen as the natural extension of the other."[3] Writing in the context of the Palestinian/Israeli conflict, Ateek argues that the justice of Israeli courts is lopsided and works against Palestinians because the Israeli Supreme Court is unwilling to interfere with military courts that try Palestinians in the occupied territories.

Our image of Justice is a blindfolded woman holding a balanced scale. It is meant to show justice is impartial. She is sometimes called blind justice because of a perceived unwillingness to see the suffering of human beings. Kurt Vonnegut's famous story *Harrison Bergeron* is about how unjust that administered attempts at achieving perfect justice can be.

Laws and rules can be unjust. If they themselves are not, then the people who administer them can apply them in unjust ways. As Ateek says, "The search for strict justice, with its overtones of retaliation, can all too easily lower people to the level of the inhuman or even the subhuman; while the exercise of mercy and

2. Ateek, *Justice and Only Justice*, 115.
3. Ateek, *Justice and Only Justice*, 116.

reconciliation can lift them up to the level of genuinely human and even to the divine."[4]

The error of thinking we are in danger of being too merciful often covers fear or one's own need for revenge. If we can cite a scene from Shakespeare's *Henry V*, the conspirators attempt to appear as King Henry's greatest supporters by counseling him against showing too much mercy to a commoner who insulted him.[5] They go so far in hiding their own fault they argue for punishment against someone who committed a lesser crime than their crime of accepting bribes to murder the king.

Ateek's point that mercy and reconciliation bring people up to the level of being "genuinely human" should bother the conscience of Western Christians. One excuse used over and over by Westerners to destroy people from other cultures is to claim, "They do not regard human life as we do." It is an ironic statement. Who do we think of as being truly human? Do we have an image of people like us in mind when we use the word "human"? Is our image of Jesus someone like us? Yes, other people from other cultures are guilty of using people like themselves as the image of being truly human. The question remains: What makes a person genuinely human in our hearts? Does an Arab Christian priest like Naim Ateek, who is eighty-seven years old at the time of this writing, fit our image of genuinely human? Does someone like Abba Kovner, mentioned in the previous chapter, fit that description? What about someone like Judas Iscariot? Would we say such a person could potentially be genuinely human?

We can agree that mercy and reconciliation will bring a person up from what they were to who they could be. Still, do we think of ourselves as genuinely human yet? Having a disposition to righteousness (*tsedeq*) helps us deal with this question. Do we attempt to do what is right in the best way? How does having more or less power factor into our answer? Again, Father Ateek observes, "Power somehow intoxicates those who wield it and clouds their sense of right and wrong so that they can justify and

4. Ateek, *Justice and Only Justice*, 42.

5. Shakespeare, *Henry V*, act 2, scene 1.

rationalize their wicked actions."[6] Ironically, those with less power have a better chance to do right in the best way because they are not in danger of losing power or position.

When religious leaders cover up crimes to protect the institution, we are seeing a fear of the loss of power. The fear of losing power once it has been gained leads to more abuses of power. Some people will call such actions merciful for all involved since they avoid a scandal. In much the same way, politicians may claim they are bringing justice to some bad people in the world. The government's treatment of people seeking refugee status at the southern border of the United States can be excused as justice. There is no righteousness involved in these actions of those in power. Justice without righteousness is injustice while mercy without righteousness is mere sentiment.

THE ROLE OF PERSONAL RIGHTEOUSNESS

What does it mean to be personally righteous? First, we must consider that St. Paul argues that no one is truly righteous in themselves. Having help from the Holy Spirit and salvation in Christ is important. The presence of God helps us make decisions to live the life described in the Beatitudes. God being present with us is a sentiment many of us enjoy. On Christmas Eve we celebrate Immanuel—God with us. However, we cannot stop at the sentiment. Christians should be present with God. Being in God's company is more than merely feeling God near us. Christians often say they feel closer to God in surroundings that have little to do with the church. I get that. I have often felt closer to God while hiking, walking, sitting at the lake fishing, or just being still on my back porch. Such times are part of Christian spirituality, like the times Jesus called his disciples to turn aside to rest and pray. For many people these times bring a sense of personal and spiritual renewal. Speaking just for myself, these times enhance my patience with other people and everything else around me. However, I cannot

6. Ateek, *Justice and Only Justice*, 124.

claim these moments enhance my sense of personal righteousness even though they may help me act righteously in the best way.

God being with us and easing our spiritual burdens was not all that the Divine will intend for us. We are to be fellow workers with God. We can only do this when we are able to listen to God. Those who hunger and thirst for righteousness choose spiritual discipline over experience-seeking.

Bishop Reuben Job renamed Wesley's third general rule from "attend upon all the ordinances of God" to "stay in love with God."[7] Staying in love with God has to do with showing love for God. Children who are told they are loved but see little evidence of it develop a confused sense of what love is. Do we want children to have the message that love is earned? Would we want them to mistake abuse for love? Of course not. Harry Chapin's hit song "Cat's in the Cradle" is about a father who learns he is being shown the same love from his son that he demonstrated to his son. The song never asks the question, but we are left to ask about the future for the grandchild.

Loving God involves loving the people of God. We sometimes find this hard to do. Many of us feel like the Greek philosopher Diogenes the Cynic who went around with a lantern claiming to look for an honest man. We may be looking in vain for the perfect congregation to join. Recently, I saw a request from someone seeking to find a "non-judgmental" church. Some recommendations were offered. I can be very judgmental at times. Should I recommend a church I lead? Will not every church have at least one judgmental person? While I do not want to play the game of semantics on judgmentalism, are we talking about the quality of the community and how we fit into it? While most folks are looking at services a church provides, we should ask about the frequency of sacraments, the quality of spiritual formation classes, and whether their talents are of use to a congregation. As a pastor, I am rarely ever asked such questions. People may ask if the church has ever harmed me or if I am ever tempted to quit. I answer yes on both counts. The

7. Job, *Three Simple Rules*, 51.

church has also been a place of healing and comfort to me as well. Why should I walk away from that?

Developing personal righteousness is more than trying to be good. Righteous people follow Christ in ways of righteousness that seek to build, otherwise we place ourselves on the side of Diogenes the Cynic who desires to tear everything apart. We find ourselves on the way to being genuinely human.

Ateek made another assertion in his quote about mercy and reconciliation lifting people up to the level of the divine. Wesleyans speak of sanctification and "going on to perfection." Since we draw our spiritual heritage through the Anglican tradition, it is evident Father Ateek is thinking about divine love. Loving as God loves is our ultimate destiny as Christians. Our personal righteousness leads to personal holiness, which will lead us into perfect love. This path begins with mercy and reconciliation. Justice, mercy, and faith are the weightier matters of the law that Jesus scolds the Pharisees for not upholding with the smaller matters like the tithe (Matt 23:23b). Tithing alone can be made into an onerous task. The Pharisees are called hypocrites because they tithed even the herbs of mint, dill, and cumin just to show they kept the laws. Jesus accused them of neglecting the spirit of the law. The purpose of the *Torah* was to bring the tribes of Israel together into one people and to preserve the people. It continues to work that way after two thousand years. Many rabbis in Jesus' day taught about these weightier matters of the law.

We see the same spirit working among Christians who two thousand years later neglect the weightier matters of justice, mercy, and faith. It is too easy to substitute a false righteousness for a true one by turning our attention away from matters of justice, the people who are hungry and thirsty, mercy, and the goal of reconciliation in this life that reflects the goal of reconciliation into perfect divine love.

Mercy keeps justice from turning into injustice. Love is first practiced in justice, and love will always prevail and make peace among people.

4

Seeing the Divine

Blessed are the pure in heart, for they will see God. (Matt 5:8)

C. S. Lewis once said the reason the pure in heart will see God is because they are the only ones who want to see the divine.[1] He tended to hold negative views about people. James is a little more optimistic. "Draw near to God and he will draw near to you. Cleanse your hands, you sinners, and purify your hearts you double-minded" (Jas 4:8). James is open to the possibility that a person may wish to see God even if their heart is not pure. Some people might be put off by the words "pure in heart." The concept of purity has been abused by Christians in recent years. Insistence on doctrinal purity or certain standards of sexual purity have caused harm to many people. Teachers and preachers who confuse the idea of purity with conformity are the problem in these cases. Still, this confusion really illustrates a true need for purity of heart as opposed to purity according to thought police or modesty patrols. We should consider the meaning of the term.

1. Lewis, *Problem of Pain*, 145.

CLEAN AND PURIFIED

The holiness code of the book of Leviticus separates everything into one of three categories. An object, animal, or person could be either unclean, clean, or holy. When the Hebrew Bible was translated into Greek, the word we translate in the New Testament as "pure" was used to translate "clean" in the categories of holy, clean, and unclean. So, purity of heart does not necessarily mean holy. Even though Heb 12:14 says, "Follow peace with everyone and the holiness without which no one shall see God." Here "pure" could mean sincere or genuine. It could also mean purified as James uses it.

The Beatitudes are traits Christians grow toward. A person's past self is not what matters in the end. What matters is whether their consciences have been purified. "Who shall ascend the hill of the LORD? And who shall stand in the holy place? Those who have clean hands and pure hearts, who do not lift up their souls to what is false and do not swear deceitfully" (Ps 24:3-4).

The Wesleyan revival is often called a holiness movement emphasizing both personal and social holiness. It was intended more as what we would call today a renewal movement. Why the difference? Today, we think of revivals and revivalism as temporary acts of the Holy Spirit. Renewal, on the other hand, is the continuous action of God. Yet, most renewal movements tend to become isolated pockets here and there without causing any real change to the status quo. Wesleyans often were looked on with suspicion. Many clergy suspected an intention to disrupt the churches. The tragedy of renewal movements is they often cause division. The Puritan heritage of John and Charles Wesley shows in their upbringing. They also knew their parents left Puritanism behind to become part of the Church of England. Neither John nor Charles Wesley intended their renewal to end with a break from the established church.

Renewals, though, bring us back to the basic question of our faith. "How can young people keep their way pure? By guarding it according to your word. With my whole heart I seek you; do not let me stray from your commandments. I treasure your word in my heart, so that I may not sin against you" (Ps 119:9–11). How shall all people live among their neighbors? Renewal should mean renewal over every part of life. Yet, for many some actions are not pure even because they know no other way. Let's look at an extreme example from the Scriptures.

The story of Simon Magus is told in the eighth chapter of the book of Acts. He was well known in the city of Samaria where the people who followed him thought his power was a great gift from God. When the deacon Philip comes to Samaria, Simon becomes a believer and is baptized. He then stays with Philip, hoping to understand the signs and miracles the deacon performs.

The leaders of the church in Jerusalem send Peter and John to impart gifts of the Holy Spirit to the new believers in Samaria. Simon sees the apostles laying their hands on the believers, imparting the Spirit of God to them. He presents the apostles with some money to gain the power to impart the Spirit to others.

We should take note of what is happening here. Simon Magus essentially tried to apprentice with Peter to learn how to do the signs and wonders. It would be bad enough for him to ask the apostles for an ability to do certain kinds of miracles. We could see Simon, for instance, ask for the ability to cast out demons or do miraculous healings. Having those abilities would not be enough for Simon, though. He wanted to receive the power and authority of an apostle. Like all other trades, magicians charged fees for taking on apprentices. Simon is offering to pay whatever fee is required to learn what the apostles know.

Simon lost his place in the community when Philip arrived. He charged fees for whatever favors people thought his magic would bring them. Simon likely thought the apostles would soon go back to Jerusalem and wanted to be the apostle for Samaria. By doing what appeared perfectly logical given his situation and background, he got a sin named after him. Simony is the practice of buying church leadership roles. Simon sought power and authority to continue offering miracles, signs, wonders, and the Holy Spirit for money.

Peter replies to this request declaring that Simon's money should perish with him. "You have no part or share in this, for your heart is not right before God. Repent therefore of this wickedness of yours, and pray to the Lord that, if possible, the intent of your heart maybe forgiven you. For I see in you that you are in the gall of bitterness and the chains of wickedness" (Acts 8:21–23).

Church tradition holds that Simon never fully repented of his sin and fell back into his former life even though the text of Acts shows him asking Peter to pray for him. Personally, I would rather the tradition be different, but it illustrates how hard it is to break from the ways of being in which we have been trained. The life Simon Magus had always known did not require a pure heart, without which his life was bitter advantage-taking over others.

Cain also comes to mind for one who could have overcome what he assumed should be. He did not understand his problem was in his assumption. When Cain and Abel made their offerings before God, Abel brought the first-born of his flock while Cain brought from his harvest. Interpreters lose their way if they attempt to consider what is being offered on the altars as to whether the offering was pleasing to God. Some try to discover deep theological truths about the nature of sacrifice. It was not what was being sacrificed that mattered. It was the kind of person making the sacrifice. The prophet Amos makes this point better than I can.

> I hate, I despise your festivals, and I take no delight in your solemn assemblies. Even though you offer me your burnt offerings and grain offerings, I will not accept them; and the offerings of well-being of your fatted animals I will not look upon. Take away from me the noise of your songs; I will not listen to the melody of your harps. But let justice roll down like waters, and righteousness like an ever-flowing stream. (Amos 5:21–24)

Cain pouts after God shows no regard for him or his sacrifice. He is an unlikable character who puts the blame on other people because they do not like him. God goes to this childish man and explains, "If you do well, will you not be accepted? And if you do not do well, sin is lurking at the door; its desire is for you, but you must master it" (Gen 4:7). Obviously, Cain does not wish to hear that he is in any way at fault. His heart is out of place. Would God favor him if he was the only one left? Joseph's brothers had a similar thought. Getting rid of Joseph should stop his father favoring him. It did, but Jacob turned his attention and affection to Benjamin.

The plans we make for ourselves to come out on top do not often work out. Even if our plans work, they demonstrate the disposition of our hearts at the time. While Cain was able to destroy his brother, he could not erase his memory. Joseph's brothers went from hating him and selling him away from their home only to live out the end of their lives hoping to keep his favor. James referred to this approach to life as being double minded in our purposes.

SINGLE-MINDED PURPOSE

The first and greatest commandment is almost impossible to comprehend for most of us. "Hear, O Israel: The LORD is our God, the LORD alone. You shall love the LORD your God with all your heart, and with all your soul, and with all your might" (Deut 6:4–5). Think carefully about those words. We are so used to saying we are supposed to just love God and our neighbor that we lose part of the meaning of that love. "All your heart, all your soul, and all your strength" are about single-minded devotion. When Elijah asks the people of the Northern Kingdom, "How long will you go limping with two different opinions?" he is talking about their divided devotion between Ba'al and the LORD (1 Kgs 18:21b).

There are two meanings we give the word "heart." One is the blood pumping muscle in the chest cavity. The other is the center or the core of the self. The heart is the place where wisdom, will, and thought reside. Today, we are likely to say the brain or the mind for these things. But we still say the heart when we discuss our emotions, sensitivities, and our core values. We use "heart" interchangeably with the word "conscience." This heart can be corrupted by appetites, passions, and desires. If we think someone has no conscience, we are also saying that person has no heart.

A corrupt conscience is difficult to overcome. Jesus does not make it easy on us. James is also getting at the "heart" of this problem with his readers. He claims they act as though they are double-minded. Their conscience is divided against itself and at war with God.

Our hearts are engaged in a lot of endeavors. We have jobs, family obligations, civic or political associations, community activities, youth sports, clubs, and so on. They round out our lives. What takes the central focus of our lives? Following Christ. How many of these other good activities are energized by our central focus? They should all be. If we lose the central focus on following Jesus, all these other good things can become means of corrupting our consciences.

Solomon became king of Israel upon the death of David. Before the Jerusalem temple was built, he went to the principal shrine at Gibeon to worship. During one such visit early in his reign God appears to him in a dream to offer the young king whatever he wished. "Give your servant therefore an understanding mind to govern your people, able to discern between good and evil" (1 Kgs 3:9a). Because Solomon asked for wisdom, God gave him the things he did not request that most young kings might have. Solomon received riches and honor all his days. He is offered a long life if he follows all the commandments.

Solomon's wisdom and intellectual achievements are rivaled only by his military conquests and his building program. He makes many alliances with neighboring kingdoms. He builds and dedicates the magnificent temple in Jerusalem when God visits him a second time. "As for you, if you will walk before me as your father David walked, with integrity of heart and uprightness, doing according to all that I have commanded you, and keeping my statutes and ordinances, then I will establish your royal throne forever" (1 Kgs 9:4–5). But it does not happen.

Solomon, despite his wisdom, did not keep the covenant. He allowed his wealth, reputation, and success to overcome his wisdom. His marriage alliances caused him to build sanctuaries and shrines to the gods of his wives. We read in 1 Kgs 11 that Solomon began to worship a few of these gods, especially those of his vassals. Jerusalem became a shrine, a place of pilgrimage for many deities, not just the God of Israel. "And Solomon did evil in the sight of the LORD, and did not completely follow the LORD, as his father David had done." While the text here places the blame on the women he married and their places of origin, Solomon committed other sins that Samuel warned against and the law forbade. He multiplied his horses and chariots, making himself a seemingly invincible army. His father, David, may have been a man of blood, but he had nothing in his arsenal compared to Solomon. Yet, there was a greater problem.

Solomon dies leaving his son Rehoboam to reign after him. Jeroboam, the son of Nebat, came home from exile and led a delegation petitioning the new king. "Your father made our yoke heavy. Now therefore lighten the hard service and his heavy yoke he placed upon us, and we will serve you" (1 Kgs 12:4). The king took three days to consider the proposal. He first asked his father's advisors what should be done. These men knew the actions of Solomon had laid heavy burdens on the people. They counseled restraint in his response.

Rehoboam then asked the men of his age group who were now his advisors. Their advice was to remind the petitioners that the king was in charge. Christians would do well to consider what this means when we only listen to our friends. The algorithms that operate social media are designed to send us information we would consider favorable to ourselves. The information could be advertising or other content we think is agreeable. The algorithms give us two bad impressions. The first is that there are many (and possibly the majority) who agree with us. When we have no interaction with people who have different points of view, we lose needed correctives to our perspectives. The second bad impression is that we begin thinking of truth as an extension of ourselves. It is important to know and recognize the truth when we see it. When we think of truth as something that gives us a vague notion of satisfaction within our minds, we are corrupted in our hearts.

Jesus claimed the truth is freeing from the slavery of self-indulgence and attitudes of superiority (John 8:31–36). The gift of having a pure heart is this knowledge of truth that frees us to follow him.

Jesus told Pilate, "Everyone who belongs to the truth listens to my voice." Pilate replied with an infamous question, "What is truth?" (John 18:37b–38). Jesus had not challenged Pilate. Yet, Pilate felt challenged. Even though John's Gospel does not mention Pilate washing his hands before sending Jesus to his death, we could almost picture Pilate dwelling on this moment and this question every time he washed his hands. Did he imagine the blood of Jesus and others he killed? Did he dry his hands on a towel each time asking himself the question, "What is truth?" What was Jesus saying to him that day?

Pilate knew the truth of his life and explained it to Jesus, "Do you refuse to speak to me? Do you not know that I have power to release you, and power to crucify you?" (John 19:19b). Really? Is there truth from power? Or does power come from truth? Pilate's exercise of power is curious. He attempts to give those accusing Jesus a little blood. He has Jesus flogged and mocked. After this humiliation, he brings Jesus out again to show what he has done. Behold the degraded man! This display is not enough to satisfy those who are threatening to become an uncontrollable mob. The taste of blood apparently left them wanting more. How does Pilate's vaunted power work after all is said and done? He tells Jesus that he holds the power of life and death, but he hears the words that make that a lie. "You would have no power over me unless it had been given you from above; therefore the one who handed me over to you is guilty of a greater sin" (John 19:11b). What does from above mean?

Pilate knows he serves at the pleasure of the emperor. Tiberius Caesar wants his empire to have peace, with revenues continuing to flow into his coffers. Does Pilate believe there is greater authority than the emperor for this world? Tiberius's adopted father, Augustus, only became immortal after he died. John says Pilate wants to release Jesus. Then another group of voices reminds him of his place in the world.

"If you release this man, you are no friend of the emperor" (John 19:12b). Forget violent mobs. An official complaint will be filed against Pilate if he releases a man claiming kingship. There, in imperial power, rests Pilate's truth. Jesus claims those who know the truth hear his voice. Pilate hears the voices of the ones accusing Jesus.

People who are not pure in heart let other issues in life get in the way of the Way. Pilate is a great example of the kind of mediocrity through which evil works. It is difficult to imagine ourselves in this story because we want to be the hero. We want to say we would never have given in to the professional blackmail of Jesus' accusers. Yet, if we truly knew ourselves, we would think twice about making such claims. Peter boasts he would die with Jesus if that is what it would take. Peter did not live up to his boasting. Fear of being also accused and condemned overcame his wish to defend.

PURIFYING ONE'S HEART

It may seem strange to begin this section with a story about King Saul. We know having a pure heart was not his best attribute, but his heart was pure toward God at the very beginning of his reign. His downfall was fear, which was also evident at the very beginning.

Saul was proclaimed king by Samuel the prophet and acclaimed by most of the Israelites. However, it was not a happy occasion. Samuel scolds the people for rejecting their God in asking for a king, and some Israelites refused to accept him as their king. Saul did not appear to the people immediately. He tried hiding first. After being proclaimed king and receiving instructions about the expected duties of the king, he returns to his father's lands.

Nahash, the king of the Ammonites, besieged the town of Jabesh-gilead. When Saul hears the news, "The Spirit of God came upon him in power . . . and his anger was greatly kindled" (1 Sam 11:6). Once Saul defeats Nahash, the victorious Israelites now recognize him as their king and decide to execute the people who would not accept Saul earlier. "But Saul said, 'No one shall be put to death this day, for today the LORD has brought deliverance to Israel'" (1 Sam 11:13). In both cases the Spirit of God is with Saul and helped him overcome his fear. He went to war and returned to show mercy. Nothing at the time made Saul feel he was going to lose his life or the respect of the people. When Samuel takes the tribes to Gilgal again, Saul's coronation is celebrated by all Israel.

Paul says when we pray the Spirit of God prays with us. "Likewise the Spirit helps us in our weakness; for we do not know how to pray as we ought, but that very spirit intercedes with sighs too deep for words. And God, who searches the heart, knows what is in the mind of the Spirit, because the Spirit intercedes for the saints according to the will of God" (Rom 8:26–27). The Divine Presence does this because the Spirit is already with the believer. "In him you also, when you had heard the word of truth, the gospel of your salvation, and had believed in him, were marked with the seal of the promised Holy Spirit; this is the pledge of our inheritance toward redemption as God's own people, to the praise of his glory" (Eph 1:13–14).

The human heart requires the work of the Holy Spirit to purify it as part of our redemption before God. The Eastern Orthodox churches practice anointing with oil as part of the baptism ritual. The anointing with holy oil symbolizes the seal of the Holy Spirit whose presence shows the child of God is due to receive the promised inheritance from the Father.

Looking back at the distinctions made between unclean, clean, and holy in Leviticus we see how our salvation is worked out in the divine sight. Baptism symbolizes the person is made clean or purified in Christ. The presence of the Spirit with each believer begins the sanctification of the person. Reflecting the perfect love of God is hope.

The Pentecostal and Charismatic movements rightly critiqued both the mainline and evangelical Protestants for ignoring the work of the Spirit. Historically, our American individualized idealism replaced the importance of the work of the Spirit for individual salvation, responsible living, and good deeds. There is nothing wrong with these ideas, but we have all apparently forgotten, like King Saul, the Godlike virtues of faith, hope, and love as well as collectively bringing glory to the name of Christ.

THE HEART AND MIND OF CHRIST

Christians would all agree that Jesus demonstrated purity of heart. Yet our theology of Jesus as the *logos* or Word of God trips us here. After all, Jesus was different from us, or so we are tempted to argue. We begin early seeing Jesus as other than we are. The Christmas song "Away in a Manger" includes the words "The cattle are lowing the baby awakes, but little Lord Jesus, no crying he makes." It is not common for infants, when their sleep is disturbed by loud noises, to keep quiet after being startled awake. Yet, we sing this difference into our perception of the little Lord Jesus every year. No wonder it is hard to consider how Jesus can relate to us in our temptations, our individual psychologies, and our cultural acclimation.

I do not believe we should give up singing "Away in a Manger." We should think about the impact some ideas have in our culture. The latter part of the song quoted above is interesting theologically. "I love thee, Lord Jesus, look down from the sky and stay by my cradle till morning is nigh." Children do not notice this suggestion that the resurrected Jesus from Easter is both ascended and among us either, but this idea is going into their future perception of Jesus too. Did Jesus have an advantage over us when it comes to being pure in heart? Probably so. But it was not because of the divine difference. It was because he readily saw the divine that made the difference.

When I am outside in the woods, I catch myself thinking, "I hope heaven is like this." I know I am not the only one who says that, but I never think of heaven being like sitting in a movie theater, a baseball game, or even an outdoor concert. It does not come to mind even though I can spend a lot of time doing those things in this life. The Beatitude promises the pure in heart will see God. It does not say where we will do that. We can assume heaven, but our doctrine teaches that the people who first heard this Beatitude were seeing God in the one who was teaching it. Purity of the heart has a lot to do with ignoring a lot of distractions while actively doing something—like when I am in the woods. That is when we see the divine at work around us.

One person told me when she was alone and cleaning the church, she would have a sudden urge to pray. Such times can come over us when we are practicing single-mindedness. They are times of contentment and happiness. To have those times, distractions need to be removed. To make those times more than momentary feelings, mental distractions need to be removed.

Early in the Sermon on the Mount, Jesus offers methods of removing mental distractions based on the commandments from laws of Moses. He uses the formula "you have heard it said . . . but I say to you" in each case. Jesus uses commandments regarding murder, adultery, oath taking, retribution, and neighbors and enemies. He ends this section with "be perfect, therefore, as your heavenly Father is perfect" (Matt 5:21–46).

Murder is a terrible crime. Every Christian agrees with this point, but many Christians are guilty of saying in moments of anger, "Someone ought to kill . . ." some terrible person who did something evil. There are Christians who undertake the murders of other people. We can argue that "real Christians" do not do those things. Yet, many Christians are willing to shout and scream at other people, calling them murderers, baby-killers, pedophiles, and evil. Jesus makes a clear point about such name-calling. Angry words and phrases spewed out upon a perceived enemy have a dehumanizing effect upon those saying them and those hearing them. They do not necessarily have intended ill effects on those to whom the vitriol is directed. I have been called lots of unflattering names and things. The only effect the name-calling has is to make me want to fight just as hard on the same terms, which is wrong.

Calling a brother or sister an idiot or fool does not make them either one. But it can produce unloving feelings for both the speaker and the victim. The proper boundaries are crossed, and new lines are drawn in a new way of connecting. We become us and them. The person I seek to fight draws allies into the foray just as I do. Engaging in this type of behavior makes us foolish.

The book of Proverbs offers an apparently contradictory couplet. "Do not answer fools according to their folly, or you will be a fool yourself. Answer fools according to their folly, or they will be wise in his own eyes" (Prov 26:4–5). Once the argument begins this behavior only gets worse. Escalating the argument does not improve behavior in any way.

How do we end such a conflict? The only way to end conflict is to admit first where our own side has done wrong without recriminations of "Well, you did worse . . . ." Reconciliation with others is important for our God who exists in the community of the Trinity. We are told our sacrificial offerings do not mean as much if we are not willing to reconcile. A pragmatic consideration to any dispute is, if we remove the issue from our own hands and leave it to, say, a judge in a court of law, even though we have assured ourselves we are right, the judge may not see it that way. It is better to reconcile without the courts or arbiters being involved.

A friend once claimed his wife told him when it came to other women "to look but don't touch." Many spouses consider adultery as the ultimate act of betrayal. For many of them the only other betrayal close to that is misusing the family savings. The problem of "look but do not touch" is we are euphemizing the idea of "desire and fantasize all you want, just don't do anything about it."

Jesus, on the other hand, uses some of the strongest language in the Sermon on the Mount concerning adultery. If your right eye is the cause of your sin, pluck it out. If your right hand causes you to sin, cut it off. We have heard the typical punishment for theft in some countries is to remove the guilty person's right hand. It serves as a symbol that the thief has stopped stealing. I suppose it is a warning to others as well.

Jesus is engaging in hyperbole here. He intentionally overstates what a person should choose to do to avoid sin. The human eye factors much into Jesus' ethic in the Sermon on the Mount. His followers should not be hypocrites who notice the speck in someone else's eye without doing something about the log in their own.

Before he gets to that example, Matthew gives another teaching that makes sense of this matter of tearing out an eye. "The eye is the lamp of the body. So, if your eye is healthy, your whole body will be full of light; but if your eye is unhealthy, your whole body will be full of darkness. If then the light in you is darkness, how great is the darkness!" (Matt 6:22–23). If your heart and mind comprehend nothing but darkness, then what good is your eye? We might see the speck in our neighbor's eye only because we are looking for it. Jesus moves away from the hyperbole of the extraction of the right eye or the right hand to a more personal and stickier subject.

The question of divorce and remarriage is avoided by most Christians. Divorce, though, is both personal and public. For that reason, we try to make the issue less public. Divorce, as said above, is often caused by sexual or financial unfaithfulness. Yet, Jesus claims, in his day at least, that divorce is the cause of adultery. He uses the specific example of a divorced woman. Husbands got divorces from wives. Wives could not get divorces. If a husband decides to legally drop his wife, he puts the stigma on her. It is assumed something is wrong with the former wife. The law in Deuteronomy regarding giving a wife a certificate of divorce is vague. The husband must find something about her that is obnoxious or objectionable (Deut 24:1–4). The onus is on the jilted wife. If she remarries and the second husband divorces her, the first husband may not remarry her because she has been "defiled." The wife bears the burden of becoming something less than what she would have been in a happy marriage. If the first divorce was an abuse of power, then the former wife will not become subject to such abuse again. A person pure of heart would not engage in this or any kind of spousal abuse.

Matthew provides more teachings from Jesus regarding marriage and divorce in later chapters. Here in the Sermon on the Mount he moves from the topic of adultery, which is an example of breaking one's promise, or having integrity regarding our words.

The late comedian Jerry Clowers would interject into his stories the phrase "If I am lying, I'm dying." Of course, it was a fabricated tale. The claim increased the humor of the story because the audience *knew* he was lying. They went along with the persona of the storyteller, which was also a fabrication.

We all know the type of person who tells lies that are hurtful and not humorous who adds an oath to what they are saying. "I swear on my mother's grave," for instance. I once heard a person claim that she would swear "on a stack of Bibles." There are other statements people without integrity use to try fooling others. We do not like people who swear falsely or habitually go back on their word. We can become so frustrated with someone that we tell the person we would rather not hear them make lying promises. Even while writing this, I can just about hear the rebuttal, "No, I mean it this time."

The phrase "so help me God" is ubiquitous in our society. I think about the commandment where we are not to "misuse the name of the LORD." We continue living in the world of contracts, bank accounts, and other parts of our society where we legally bind ourselves by giving our signature. Could it be that the latter is more in keeping with Jesus' teaching than any oath we take?

Jesus uses heaven and earth and the city of Jerusalem as places that do not belong to the people who take oaths swearing by them. Jesus says we should merely keep our word. Expecting a person to take an oath or sign a loyalty pledge is a way of saying we do not trust the person we are binding. We wish to assess a penalty if the person refuses to honor the oath. The pure in heart are people who can be trusted.

A common oath that is taken is the vow to get vengeance for a wrong. We catch ourselves making outlandish promises such as "I swear to track the culprit down to the ends of the earth." When a terrible outrage has been done to an innocent child, we may claim that "hanging is too good for them." I recall when the Oklahoma City bomber, Timothy McVeigh, was about to be executed for killing 186 people in a domestic terrorist attack on the Murrah building, many people in the congregations I served were ready for him to die. What he did was evil, but I could see little justice in his execution.

The *lex talonis*, which is eye for an eye, tooth for a tooth, and life for a life, is misused by many Christians to justify revenge. It was designed to curb revenge. The law regulates what retaliation is allowed.[2]

Jesus then enters into what is the most controversial teaching in the Sermon. He says we should not seek revenge for anything we have lost. If anything, Jesus tells us to give more than they demand. We will discuss this teaching more in the next chapter.

God makes the sun rise on the evil people as well as the good people. Jesus tells his followers that God gives the basic gifts of life to them and those same gifts to those who are arrayed against them. Should his followers treat people worse than his Father treats them? When we look at those people who abuse us, do we wish to be like them?

Jesus says even a tax collector has friends. Are we committed to love only our friends? If we selectively greet only those who we consider family, how are we different from the rest of the world?

Being selective in these ways causes more problems than we are willing to admit. We tend to view our friends, family, and church members as more important to us and better than other people. When they let us down in some way, we tend to be more apt to defend them because they are our friends. If my compatriot harms someone, should I simply excuse the behavior? Why should I assume my friend's crime is somehow less bad than when I learn that someone I dislike is guilty of the same thing? Jesus' words "but I say to you" change our perspective of what loving our neighbor means in context with loving God.

Becoming pure in heart sounds like an impossible goal. Of course, so does seeing the Divine one who lives in unapproachable light, yet both can happen. We have some self-work to do so our hearts may be purified. The first step is to regain our focus on Jesus, his way, and his teaching. The next step is to let that focus inform our other commitments. The third step is to let the healing begin. As our hearts are purified, we will find it easier to be peacemakers.

2. See chapter 2.

5

Children of the Divine One

Blessed are the peacemakers, for they will be called
the children of God. (Matt 5:9)

THE WORD "PEACEMAKERS" SHOWS up only once in the New Testament. It is a compound word made from the word for peace and a word that means "to do, make, commit, cause, work, perform, etc." It gets the attention of a lot of people who try to nail down the meaning. Both mercy and forgiveness are involved with peacemaking. Peacemakers do not necessarily have peace. They have the distinction of being children of God who demonstrates mercy and forgiveness. Let's consider a story from American history.

Dr. Benjamin Rush believed in dreams. He dreamed in 1809 of John Adams writing a letter of reconciliation to Thomas Jefferson. He told the former president, who did nothing about it. A few years later, Dr. Rush tried again at Christmas. He wrote to Adams about a conversation he had with Jefferson, "And now my dear friend, permit me again to suggest to you to receive the olive branch offered to you by the hand of a man who still loves you." On New Year's Day 1812, Adams wrote a letter to Jefferson. Who was the peacemaker in the story? All the men in the story were.

Why? Mercy and forgiveness were offered and accepted by every-one involved.[3]

Mercy is very important in making peace, but a false mercy makes a false peace. "Because from the least to the greatest ev-eryone is greedy for unjust gain; from prophet to priest everyone deals falsely. They have treated the wound of the daughter of my people carelessly, saying, 'Peace, peace,' when there is no peace" (Jer 8:10b–11). Overlooking harm that has been caused is not mercy. Forgiveness is not saying, "what you did is acceptable behavior." Mercy is deciding not to retaliate for what was done.

Drama is often fueled by the desire to retaliate. A friend's fa-ther got tired of hearing his children argue about who owed what to whom. In his frustration, he declared, "Jubilee, all debts are can-celed." After a while, his children could no longer remember what was owed. A Baptist congregation I know once had a group split off to form another church, and then another group left to join another church. One of the deacons proposed sending each group a check of so many thousand dollars each with a letter blessing them and their future works. They did not follow through with it. But I was impressed with the wisdom in suggesting such a move. Would that go a long way to reconciling the hurt feelings involved and making peace? I believe it would have.

Mercy and peacemaking require us to do something we do not want to do. We stop retaliating for hurts that have been caused. Recovery programs eventually ask the participants to make a list of every person they have harmed and to offer some kind of amends. It is tempting to believe that suffering people would be ready to do that. Usually, it is not that easy. What they do instead is ask for three lists. One list is for everyone you believe you can apologize too. The second list is for everyone you do not know how to make amends to. And the third list is for everyone with whom you are so angry that you never intend to make amends. Those are the people we swear, "I will see them in hell before I ever speak to them again."

Peacemaking requires mercy, forgiveness, and a spirit of reconciliation. These requirements are needed between nations

3. McCullough, *John Adams*, 603.

and nationalities as well as individuals. The ingredients of peace, though, do not make peace without a willingness to pursue peace. The writer of Hebrews calls for the reader to "pursue peace with everyone" (Heb 12:14a). Paul says, "If it is possible, so far as it depends on you, live peaceably with all" (Rom 12:18). A. J. Muste, the founder of the Fellowship of Reconciliation, is often quoted for saying, "There is no way to peace; peace is the way."[4] It is almost cliché to use it here, but that is only because we tend to think of peace in one or two ways. The first is the absence of conflict. The second is when we think of peace as the cessation of conflict.

Peace as the absence of conflict is often an Edenic ideal in our minds. Nothing bad happens. We think we can have enough food for everyone to be greedy if they wish. Every animal does our bidding, and we are not required to do anything we do not wish to do.

Wait, you say that is not how we picture Paradise? Who cleans up after the animals? Where do all the seeds, pits, and rinds of the food everyone eats go? Do we picture a chicken offering itself for our evening meal? Thinking of peace as the absence of conflict sets up an impossibility of living in our minds.

Many of us living today remember the signing of the Camp David Accords that led to a treaty of peace between Israel and Egypt. The peace agreement made by Egyptian President Anwar Sadat and Israeli Prime Minister Menachem Begin ended some territorial disputes that had resulted from three wars involving Israel and its Arab neighbors. In our general experience, we may be forgiven for thinking of peace in terms of the absence of conflict or the cessation of conflict.

The image of the mediator getting the photo op of persuading opposing leaders to shake hands as if in friendship is a feel-good moment, but neither a handshake nor a signature on a document really makes peace. As the Versailles Treaty of 1918 demonstrates, at best it was an agreed armistice—a cease-fire agreement. The treaty did not bring peace to Europe. Peace has yet to be brought to Europe, but several conflicts are being managed by a lot of people

---

4. "Debasing Dissent," 46.

to prevent animosity among neighboring countries from escalating into bloodshed.

What makes for peace?

Peace is a form of action.

Dr. David Graybeal had long been retired from Drew University when I met him. He was still every inch the theology professor and enjoyed monthly meetings with pastors who discussed a lot of issues with him. Not only was he a teacher, he was also a World War II veteran of the U.S. Navy. When the subject of reconciliation was discussed, he offered a story from his wartime experience.

Dr. Graybeal was a crew member on a ship that was dropping depth charges on a U-boat in the North Atlantic. The German submarines at the time were destroying supply and troop ships to Britain. The depth charges kept the submarine from firing torpedoes at them. Suddenly the U-boat surfaced and using the signal lamp flashed in Morse code the English words "Going down. Pick up my crew." Then the hatches opened for the submariners to abandon their boat and swim to the American ship.

The depth charges stopped and climbing nets were sent over the side to help the enemy sailors climb on board. Since the water was extremely cold, David and his fellow sailors wrapped the German crew in blankets and served them hot coffee and later soup. They exchanged the Germans' wet uniforms for dry clothes. They took care of them until the prisoners could be sent to America.

"We spent three days with them and were sorry to see them go. Wasn't that an example of reconciliation?" he asked the group. To go from trying to destroy a submarine and kill everyone on board to saving their lives is reconciliation in some sense. Paul quotes, "If your enemies are hungry feed them; if they are thirsty, give them something to drink; for by doing this you will heap burning coals on their heads" (Rom 12:20; cf. Prov 25:21–22). The phrase "heap burning coals on their heads" has many potential meanings. One is judgment. Another is the enemy feeling sorrowful. And one possibility is that the heap of coals means giving warmth. No matter the meaning of the phrase, it is possible the way Paul uses it, he means the enemy is no longer an enemy. The story the professor told us gives one the impression that we heap the burning coals on our own heads as well.

Dr. Graybeal's story reminded me of a similar one told me by a church member who was a veteran of the Italian campaign during the same war. He said, "When we showed up, those Italians were pulling hams out of hollowed out stumps and wine and bread from trees where they had hidden them. The Germans had told them the American soldiers were starving and coming to steal their food. They really believed we were starving."

He believed the Italian people saw the Americans as welcome liberators. Perhaps they did. On the other hand, the people could have thought of the Americans as another occupier like the Germans. Mussolini had declared war on the United States in 1941. It could be the Italians were attempting to welcome an enemy. Being hospitable to an enemy is unusual, but people who are tired of fighting and tired of bullies with guns stealing their resources will figure out how to live in harmony with other people.

A newcomer to a church I once served spoke to the senior minister. "I have been part of many congregations, but this is the first one where the members are not fighting each other."

The minister responded, "This congregation fought for the last thirty years until they got sick of it."

The word "sick" stuck with me. The conversation was at the beginning of the first war against Iraq. I asked myself then and now, "What would happen if the people of the world realized that constant fighting is unhealthy?"

We read in the previous chapter how the pure in heart will not seek revenge for what is lost. Rather, they will seek for justice in the opposite direction. After telling his followers to "turn the other cheek," Jesus goes on to say, "and if anyone wants to take your coat, give your cloak as well; and if anyone forces you to go one mile, go also the second mile" (Matt 5:40–41). Galilee, Samaria, and Judea all lived under Roman occupation. The people were subject to Roman laws. Jesus tells his listeners to obey the laws and rulings and then freely commit to doing more. For most people, attempting to avoid doing the bare minimum of what we are required to do makes sense. When Jesus is confronted with the question "Is it lawful to pay taxes to Caesar?" he uses the image on the coin, claiming what has Caesar's image rightly belongs to Caesar (Matt 22:15–22). In other words, let Caesar and the empire have *everything* that belongs to them. God requires everything that belongs to God.

A popular story about St. Francis tells how his father, Pietro Bernadone, took him to court to have the law enforce his son's obedience to him. His father claimed that everything Francis owned he got from him, including the clothes he wore. At this point, the young man took his clothes off, folded them neatly, gave them to his father, and left the court naked as the day he was born.[5] Did this action heap the metaphorical coals of fire on his father's head?

Peacemaking means making a sacrifice of some kind on everyone's part to make reconciliation possible. Some sacrifices are larger than others. Menachem Begin of Israel had to give up the Sinai Peninsula for peace with Egypt. Anwar Sadat lost allies and friends for peace with Israel.

President Carter claimed during a lecture I attended that, in situations of civil war, the Carter Center tries to get both sides to agree to free elections. Part of the agreement is for each party to live by the results. Since both sides often believe they will win, getting an agreement to hold an election can be easy. Getting each side to agree, if the observers agree the election has been fair, to live by the results is a test of their character. Will those making peace keep their word? It is curious how much human suffering or thriving is based on the character of people. It is true on the large scale of nations and the small scale of individuals and families. What about making peace in churches?

PEACEMAKING IN THE CHURCH

The special-called annual conference regarding disaffiliations made me anxious. I did not want to be there. I hoped there would

5. Chesterton, *Life of Saint Francis.*

be no debate that would make matters worse, but I was never going to be fully mentally or emotionally prepared for the vote. So, I did not vote. However, the vote was overwhelmingly in favor of releasing the congregations who wanted to leave. There were a few no votes. I do not know if there were any others who abstained.

My chosen church—I am not a cradle United Methodist—was separating over what exactly? Human sexuality, biblical authority, failure to uphold the Book of Discipline are all reasons that are given. The overall conclusion is the final question either to be "inclusive" or "exclusive." These words possess no meaning by themselves but only together as contradictions. For some reason, though, they brought out the worst in some of us, which made many others angry. The conclusion was neither side would budge, and we were tired of fighting.

Peacemaking is better than trying to get our own way. We think that we know what is best. We try to persuade and cajole others to our way of thinking. They, on the other hand, believe we are wrong. So, they try to persuade and cajole others to their way of thinking. Unless we reach some agreement recognizing we are fallible human beings intending to work things out, we will continue to laud ourselves and complain that the other is deceived, untruthful, and in the thrall of the devil. Suddenly, we are in the position of escalating accusations like Job's three friends. It may sound dramatic, but this is how polarization works. In such situations, people do not lose, they get to think of themselves as martyrs for what is right. We find ways to oppose the very idea of peacemaking and yet call ourselves "the children of God."

Church institutions find themselves in lawsuits over problems of their own creation. The sexual abuse scandal in the Roman Catholic Church opened the door for churches to be sued and to sue each other. Holding an institution civilly accountable for such negligence is just. Churches suing each other is not seeking justice. Yet, we have plenty of evidence that this is nothing new. We see this behavior in the Scriptures as well.

Paul's enemies took him to the court of the proconsul Gallio in Corinth. They accused Paul of "teaching people to worship God contrary to the law." Gallio refused to allow the accusers to have standing in his court to bring such charges. "If it were a matter of some villainy, I would be justified in accepting the complaint of you Jews; but since it is a matter of questions about words and names and your own law, see to it yourselves." (Acts 18:14b–15b). When writing to the Corinthian church about how the members resorted to the same law courts to settle disputes, Paul says, "In fact, to have lawsuits at all with one another is already a defeat for you. Why not rather be wronged? Why not rather be defrauded? But you yourselves wrong and defraud—and believers at that!" (1 Cor 6:7–8). Courts of law do not make peace among people—they simply provide settlements for disputes. One will still find people involved in the suit who are unhappy with the ruling because either the judge ruled against them or did not give them enough recompense. If the law does not make peace, then what does?

Human beings make peace. There is no other way of conducting ourselves but to make peace. The minister of the church where I was raised once quoted this Beatitude and then added, "not the peace lovers." I am not sure what he meant. Did he mean people who protested the nuclear arms race? Was he referring to the people who protested the possible American intervention in Nicaragua? These are the places where my mind went. I am not sure about his mind. Suppose though, he meant that there are people who wish for peace but will do nothing about it. We cannot understand why people will not get along and work together. Yet, we do not seek to understand why there is grievance in the first place.

Naim Ateek, who is mentioned in a previous chapter, claims the church in the Middle East has "a dual imperative" of being prophetic and making peace. He writes of his specific Palestinian context. Reverend Munther Isaac gave a powerfully prophetic Christmas sermon in 2023 called "Jesus in the Rubble" that called out the complicity of the Western church in the genocide of the Palestinian people.[6] I am inclined to agree that wherever the church is the context calls for both a prophetic witness and peacemaking work. Living in peace is to live prophetically.

6. Isaac, "Christ in the Rubble.'"

Tolstoy told many stories. One tale called "Walk in the Light While You Have Light" is one of the most interesting. It tells of an early convert to Christianity who lives a life of peace and harmony so that when he dies, he barely notices the change from life to new life.[7] When I look back on my own thoughts of what I hope heaven is, it does not occur to me I really do not live my life in those wild places. Those places are a break in my existence. To live as a hermit in the wilderness would take nothing less than a call from God to do it. If I want my life to reflect the life of heaven, I must live it that way. As Tolstoy also observed, "It turns out that nobody can live well, but that we may only talk about it."[8]

The Beatitudes are gifts for living the heavenly way—the blessed life, if you will. Bringing peace to the church is the first place we begin in making peace in the world. What happens when we pursue peace with our neighbor who sits one row over from us? What do we fear? Rejection? Or do we fear losing something else? This question is sticky when members of our own families are involved. Do we want to be considered disloyal to family?

It is commonplace in many churches to find a family where no one makes a move without the permission of another family member. No one wants to make Sunday dinner any more uncomfortable than it already is. Peacemaking is not allowed when an authority figure holds a grudge. At some point, we must decide to make peace and not hold someone else's grudges. It can be done.

PEACE WITH JUSTICE

A common chant for protests during the last part of the twentieth century was framed as a threat or—perhaps we could say—a promise, "No Justice. No Peace." While I understand the basic idea that peace without justice is neither peace nor justice, the negative formula is unfortunate. People should commit to peace when seeking justice. Peaceable living is just and righteous living.

---

7. Tolstoy, *Walk in the Light*.

8. Tolstoy, *Walk in the Light*, 8.

If our commitment is to peaceful coexistence with our neighbors, then we follow the golden rule. When we find ourselves the only one living this way, we can say with the psalmist, "Too long have I had my dwelling among those who hate peace. I am for peace; but when I speak, they are for war" (Ps 120:6–7). Violent actions reflect incompetence and weakness. Resorting to violent ways means humans fail to accomplish justice and peace. We have been incompetent in our efforts and decided resorting to force is the only way to accomplish our goals.

A white man from South Africa and I were classmates at one time. When the policy of apartheid was ending in the first national election that enfranchised black voters, he smoldered while the rest of us thought what was happening in his country was a great and joyful moment. When asked about the election, he replied, "Name one African country that isn't one hundred years behind in development." His anger was born of fear. He was afraid what was going to happen next when "the blacks take over" as he saw it.

The major South African political parties involved had already made a peaceful transition to power their primary goal. Knowing the black majority would demand their oppressors be brought to justice, all sides had to consider how that would happen. Many white South Africans were familiar with stories of violent gangs of black people, including members of Winnie Mandela's infamous "United Football Club." Who would hold them accountable for their crimes?

One method almost immediately dismissed from consideration was a series of trials much like the Nuremburg trials of the leaders of Nazi Germany. Desmond Tutu observed, "The whole process left a simmering resentment in many Germans."[9] A victor's justice is one-sided. Nor could an approach of saying all is in the past while we move forward happen. Memories are always in the present for the victims. The need for peace, though, ran much deeper than even the leaders of South Africa suspected.

---

9. Tutu, *No Future Without Forgiveness*, 20.

All South Africans were less than whole than we would have been without apartheid. Those who were privileged lost out as they became more uncaring, less compassionate, less humane, and therefore less human; for this universe has been constructed in such a way that unless we live in accordance with its moral laws we will pay a price for it. One such law is that we are bound together in what the Bible calls "the bundle of life." Our humanity is caught up in that of others. We are human because we belong. We are made for community, for togetherness, for family, to exist in a delicate network of interdependence . . . . We are brothers and sisters of one another whether we like it or not and each one of us is precious individual.[10]

Many have paid the price for failing to live in accordance with these universal laws. Oppressors, as we just read, lose their humanity as they dehumanize the people they subjugate. The South Africans chose a truth and reconciliation process. The process itself further exposed the woundedness of all the people. Acknowledging wounds in ourselves and other people leads to healing. Unacknowledged wounds do not heal properly, if at all.

Are there other ways to seek justice by peaceful means? It is impossible without truth, which is difficult to get sometimes. Yet, to live peaceably requires acknowledging what is true. "So then, putting away all falsehood, let all of us speak the truth to our neighbors, for we are members of one another" (Eph 4:25). We see truth abused almost every day of our lives. We live in a world of lies, falsity, and misdirection. We are tempted to ask with Pilate, "What is truth?" It is not as difficult as it may seem. We may have to reevaluate how much of what we hear is truth and how much are simply words with which we agree. It is easy to fall into the trap of listening to what we wish to think. This temptation is the main reason we do not get history correct. We want to believe words that make us into something special.

A favorite episode of *The Andy Griffith Show* deals with the history of the town of Mayberry—particularly a great heroic battle

---

10. Tutu, *No Future Without Forgiveness*, 196–97.

that is part of the founding myth. Opie must write an essay on the battle. Many of the citizens of Mayberry want to tell him about the role their ancestors played in the victory. He finds that almost all of them claim their ancestor was a colonel of the militia and the hero of the battle. Since the battle was against the local Native Americans, Andy and Opie go to a Native American man who claims his ancestors won the battle and drove the settlers away.

Realizing that all these stories cannot be true, Andy and Opie dig a little into some out-of-town newspapers and learn what actually took place. While the intention to fight was there at the beginning, there had been no battle. Instead, both sides reached an agreement and had a big party. When the men returned to their families, they concocted the tales of a glorious military victory.

Telling the truth did not endear Sheriff Andy and his son to their fellow citizens. When asked about the response of his school friends, Opie replied, "It seems they all had colonels in their families too."[11] The lie was about a battle. The truth was about reconciliation. But the participants had been too embarrassed to tell the truth, which when it came out embarrassed their descendants. However, the truth was a better story *because* it was true. We can be embarrassed by the truth, but it frees us so that we may become pure in heart and thereby live peacefully with our neighbors.

The prophetic work of the church is telling the truth in love. It is right to stand for justice. It is just to stand for righteousness. But as we saw in an earlier chapter having righteousness or justice without mercy misses the goal. Again, that goal is healing.

HEALING

The Gospels all contain stories about Jesus healing people. Some of the stories are about Jesus healing individuals of illnesses like paralysis, blindness, or other chronic and apparently incurable conditions. Yet some others are about his healing demonically possessed people. Christians have differing opinions about these

11. Rakin, "Battle of Mayberry."

miracles. Do they happen today? Were they only in the past? Did not ancient people mistake mental illness for demonic influence? A person may be skeptical about these stories and still learn valuable lessons.

One such story is when Jesus returns from the Mount of Transfiguration with three of his disciples to find a man in distress over his son who is apparently possessed. Jesus learns his disciples cannot cast the evil spirit out of the boy. Now that the teacher has arrived, the father asks Jesus, "If you are able to do anything have pity on us and help us." Jesus is surprised by the lack of faith shown by both the disciples and the father. Why bring the boy to him if he did not believe anything could be done for him? "Jesus said to him, 'If you are able!—All things can be done for the one who believes.' Immediately the father of the child cried out, 'I believe; help my unbelief!'" (Mark 9:23–24). Once the offending demon is cast out of the boy, Jesus and his disciples discuss the matter privately. The disciples want to know, "Why could we not cast it out?" Jesus replies, "This kind can only come out with prayer" (Mark 9:29).[12]

We should consider the elements required for this healing. Faith and prayer (with or without fasting) are a combination of virtue and discipline. Peacemaking requires the same combinations of virtues with disciplines. Faith, hope, and love are called the *theological virtues* because, like God, they are creative in nature. As every artist, athlete, soldier, engineer, and architect knows there can be no creation or beauty without discipline.

Eberhard Arnold spent his youth studying the Bible and the classic Christian work *The Imitation of Christ*. His studies led him outside of official Christendom into the Anabaptist tradition. He became convinced that Christian living meant living in community. He and his wife Emmy founded the first *Bruderhof*—House of Brothers—in the late 1920s in Germany. When the Nazi government came to power, Arnold had a few contacts in the local government who warned him of an impending raid by the Gestapo.

---

12. The King James Bible includes the words "and fasting" at the end of the verse, which is not a bad thought when praying for spiritual strength or courage.

He prayerfully considered what he and his community could do. Eberhard asked the sisters working in the kitchen if they would bake a cake because they would be expecting guests the next day.[13]

The Gospel teachings of Jesus and a good dose of common sense left Arnold no alternative. If they chose to resist, they would meet with force resulting in imprisonment or death. Not resisting in any way was a commonsense measure. Welcoming the enemy as guest was the greater and divine way. Eventually, the Arnolds and their community moved on and settled in England. They did not live through the horrors those SS men perpetuated in the war. Two ways are shown in this story. The way of the world is shown in the extremist attitudes of the Nazi neighbors of the Arnolds. The way of peacemaking and healing leads people to peace and spiritual health.

THE MAN OF BLOOD

King David had a great idea. As he said to the prophet Nathan, "I am living in a house of cedar, but the ark of the covenant of the LORD is under a tent." Nathan thought it was a great idea too. The people would finally have a central and permanent place to worship their God in their king's city. David is a hero and the LORD's anointed. God, however, was not excited about the whole idea. Someone else will build the place David proposes. One of his sons will build it instead (1 Chr 17:1–15). Before his death, while handing over the plans to Solomon, David says, "My son, I planned to build a house to the name of the LORD my God. But the word of the LORD came to me, saying, 'You have shed much blood and have waged great wars; you shall not build a house to my name because you have shed so much blood in my sight on the earth. See, a son shall be born to you; he shall be a man of peace. I will give him peace from all his enemies on every side . . . and I will give peace and quiet to Israel in his days'" (1 Chr 22:7b–9).

Peace and worship do work together for the greater glory of God. Who gives King Solomon and Israel peace? It was not

13. "Eberhard Arnold's Life and Work."

because David had subdued his enemies. He shed too much blood to ever be considered peaceable. It will not be Solomon who gives Israel peace either, even though his wisdom will make it possible to pursue peaceful ways with his neighbor kings. The gift of peace is ultimately granted by God.

It is too easily forgotten when we try to make peace within the churches, our communities, or even among nations that the burden is not completely ours. We see the task, the necessity, and the problem. We get caught up in these attributes while forgetting the grace and love that is always present through God. David's error was he could always see the problem and the duty that accompanied it. He would not kill King Saul because the king was the Lord's anointed. David knew he had to maintain the sanctity of the anointing because it was also his claim to kingship. Killing the anointed of the LORD would be to allow disregard for every anointed of the LORD. It was not grace that motivated him.

Solomon though will not be simply the anointed of the LORD. God will adopt him. "He shall be a son to me, and I shall be a father to him, and I will establish his royal throne in Israel forever" (1 Chr 22:10). The man of peace will be the child of God.

PROMISES, PROMISES

Paul observes that the fifth commandment is the first commandment with a promise. "'Honor your father and mother'—this is the first commandment with a promise; 'so that it may be well with you and may you live long on the earth'" (Eph 6:2–3). As we have seen, all the Beatitudes contain a promise. "Blessed are the peacemakers, for they shall be called the children of God" contains a unique promise. Peacemakers are Godlike in their efforts. While we are used to calling each other the children of God, we forget how children resemble their parents. We share many attitudes, points of view, mannerisms, and heritage with our parents. We also share physical characteristics. We say a child has one parent's eyes and the other's chin, for instance. A friend once said about his family, "All of us are born with wrinkles."

How do peacemakers resemble God? We are now discussing the great gift of this Beatitude. Being children of the divine means God can be seen in us. Another friend once said to me, "We do not see souls in bodies because we see bodies through souls." How we carry ourselves, how we smile, and how we look responding to something are not things seen in dead bodies. How then, we may ask, do we see souls in God?

C. S. Lewis is best known for his Narnia books and his books of Christian apologetics. But he is less known for his Space Trilogy. These books introduce us to the character named Ransom, who undertakes adventures on dying Mars and newly enlivened Venus. In the last book, *That Hideous Strength*, he has become imbued with the sense of the Divine. After encountering him as the director of a group living in a community, Jane Studdock finds herself conflicted on three levels. And then she reaches the fourth one. "This fourth and supreme Jane was simply in the state of joy . . . she saw from the windows of the train the outlined beams of sunlight pouring over stubble or burnished woods and felt like they were the notes of a trumpet. Her eyes rested on rabbits and cows as they flitted by and she embraced them in heart with merry, holiday love."[14] Lewis claims Ransom is a living saint whose presence lingers despite Jane's initial reluctance to follow his advice. The experience Lewis describes for her is that of experiencing the soul of Ransom through the Divine one. Jane wishes for the sense of joy to continue the rest of the evening and makes some scattered plans to preserve it.

One aspect of the promises that has not yet been mentioned is the importance of obedience. Paul's discussion about the fifth commandment is in the context of instructions to obedience to parents. Jesus emphasizes obedience as well throughout the Sermon on the Mount. When he tells his followers not to worry, he gives this instruction, "But strive first for the Kingdom of God and his righteousness, and all these things will be given to you as well" (Matt 6:33). The parable of the two men who build houses, one on stone and the other on sand, illustrates this point too.

---

14. Lewis, *That Hideous Strength*, 151–52.

> Everyone who hears these word of mine and acts on
> them will be like a wise man who built his house on rock.
> The rain fell and the floods came, and the winds blew and
> beat on that house, but it did not fall, because it had been
> founded on rock. And everyone who hears these words
> of mind and does not act on them will be like a foolish
> man who built his house on sand. The rain fell, and the
> floods came, and the winds blew and beat against that
> house, and it fell—and great was its fall. (Matt 6:24–27)

Obedience comes from faith in what God will do. Jesus calls us to be peacemakers in our lives with others so people will see, like Ransom, us in God. Before we try to understand a problem, we seek the grace and love of God. We attempt to help the problem be solved in obedience to this light.

Vernard Eller tells the story of his son Enten who decided against registering for the U.S. Selective Service. Enten was clear to both his defense attorneys and the prosecutors that his decision was an act of obedience to God and not civil disobedience to the law of the land. The prosecution and the judge in the trial did not merely condemn the prisoner and move on to the next case. They were faced with a person they did not want to convict. When the press asked if he thought he had won the case, Enten Eller replied the question made no sense since there was no fight.[15]

The peacemaking of Enten Eller and many others began long before they were born. They demonstrate the attitude and obedience of Abraham's son Isaac who faced a lot of opposition from his neighbors over the wells once dug by his father. Whenever he was challenged about the water, he moved on until no one else laid claim to his work. "He moved there and dug another well, and they did not quarrel over it; so he called it Rehoboth, saying 'Now the LORD has made room for us, and we shall be fruitful in the land'" (Gen 26:22). But that was not the end of it for Isaac. The people who quarreled with him had a change of heart and offered peace. They celebrated the reconciliation and lived as neighbors should, in peace.

---

15. Eller, *Christian Anarchy*, 258–67.

6

When You Encounter the Hateful

Blessed are those who are persecuted for righteousness' sake,
for theirs is the kingdom of heaven. (Matt 5:10)

Blessed are you when people hate you, and when they exclude you,
revile you, and defame you on account of the Son of Man. Rejoice in
that day and leap for joy, for surely your reward is great in heaven;
for that is what their ancestors did to the prophets. (Luke 6:22–23)

THE EARLY CHURCH FACED many persecutions. At first, it was because they were Jewish. Later, it was because they were not Jewish
enough for Rome to consider them under the exception. Still later
the early Christians were a good group on whom everyone else
could blame their problems. Historically, there were only a few
times the persecution of Christians was empire-wide. Persecutions
happened mostly in isolated places here and there.

Jesus tells us whenever persecution comes to remember that
we are in good company. The people who persecute another people only do so when it is convenient for them. Few people go out
of their way to do it unless they think there will be some reward
for it. After my time in the former Soviet Union, I have a different perspective on the persecution many American Christians
claim to suffer. Even within denominations there are accusations
of persecution of one group against another. Yet, it usually means

one side is not getting their way, not one group burning down the buildings of another group.

Jesus gives instructions on how to deal with persecution when it does come. We are to love our enemies and pray for those who abuse us. We respond with love to their hate or indifference to our fate. Jesus was one of the few people who taught this response. When we read the Dead Sea Scrolls from the community at Qumran, we see counsel that persecuted people should destroy their persecutors. They disappeared as a community. The movement inspired by Jesus is still with us.

The teaching Jesus gave his followers allowed them to decide what to do after persecutions ended. During the persecution under the Emperor Diocletian, some Christians surrendered the Holy Scriptures and other Christian writings to be destroyed. Many renounced their faith rather than being jailed. And later, many of these same people regretted their actions and attempted to rejoin the community of believers.[1] What should be done about them? Some church leaders in northern Africa argued that such people should never be allowed to return. One can even find a justification for this belief in the New Testament. "For if we willfully persist in sin after having received the knowledge of the truth, there no longer remains a sacrifice for sins" (Heb 10:26). No grace and no mercy are allowed for people who did nothing but evil in saving their own skin. Eventually that view, known as Donatism, was declared heresy.

Instead, the orthodox believers remembered what Jesus said in the Sermon on the Mount. If we are supposed to treat our enemies with grace, then what about our fellow believers? Some who were tortured to give up their faith admitted they could not say what they would have done if the torture continued. They interceded for those who turned back, and thereby allowed for healing in the church community.

---

1. Related by my seminary professor Charles (Ted) Hackett, Candler School of Theology, 2000.

THE GOLDEN RULE

"Do to others as you would have them do to you." We just saw an example of someone doing for another person what the other person did not know they needed—someone to intercede for them.

Rabbi Hillel was an old man when Jesus was born. Legend has it that a gentile challenged him to explain the entire Jewish law while the man balanced on one foot. The sage said, "Whatever is harmful to you, do not do to another."[2] I agree with that statement. Other teachers and sages in diverse cultures have said the same thing. The first general rule of Methodists is "Do no harm," but that is not what Jesus says.

A person can go through an entire day without doing harm to anyone. The same person can also go through an entire day not doing anyone any good. The second general rule for Methodists is "Do good."

I have been in discussions with people who recognize the difference between these teachings and ask seriously if the golden rule is truly ethical. "What if," they ask, "another person does not want the good you would want?" We get the answer to that question in chapter 10 of Luke in the parable of the good Samaritan. The injured man may not have wanted a Samaritan helping him, but that good action was necessary for the man to be healed.

Jesus gives us the knowledge that people need love even when they do not understand it. Praying for enemies helps us learn to forgive them and eventually love them. It is not easily done, but Christ calls us to be healers in a world where people seek to do harm. Healing is at the heart of his work.

There are Christians who live where persecutions can break out against them at any minute. Often, though, we do not see these believers acting as though it could. Other Christians must be cautious about expressing their faith. Yet many of these, too, do not live as though they are fugitives. Instead, we see fellow believers going about their daily lives within the culture where they live. This behavior was also the practice of the early Christians.

2. From a story told me by Rabbi Erin Boxt, Temple Beth El, April 2022.

Scaring comfortable people into believing they may be persecuted at any time is a method of controlling people. Many cults use this practice to promote group cohesion. It reminds me of a telephone call I once received.

"Hello. Is this Reverend Jones?"

"It is," I replied.

"Revered Jones, I am ——, and I am calling about a Bible study program about the persecuted church . . ."[3]

I was already familiar with games about the persecuted church that were being used on youth and college students in some ministries. They involved students risking asking the wrong person about where the Christians are meeting. The program being offered during that call included a camping trip where youth were attacked by uniformed adults who are persecuting them for being Christians. Once the Bible studies primed the students to react fearfully and accept the situation as real, the greater the "lesson" would be for them.

Suffering for the faith is considered a major New Testament theme by many people. "Indeed, all who want to live a godly life in Christ Jesus will be persecuted" (2 Tim 3:12). However, if you feel you are persecuted, it does not follow you are living in godly ways. James offers advice based on the Beatitude. "As an example of suffering and patience, beloved, take the example of the prophets who spoke in the name of the Lord. Indeed we call blessed those who showed endurance. You have heard of the endurance of Job, and you have seen the purpose of the Lord, how the Lord is compassionate and merciful" (Jas 5:9–10).

A strange problem during the later first and early second centuries was Christians who actively sought to be made martyrs. Ignatius of Antioch desired to suffer martyrdom and feared the Christians in Rome would do something to interfere with him doing so. There is the legend of Eulpus who shouted to a Roman governor while he was holding court, "I am a Christian. I want to die!" The governor, so the story goes, granted his request. Clement

---

3. I tell this story in full in my recovery memoir *The Sun Still Shines: The Legend of a Drunken Pastor.*

of Rome warns against voluntarily turning oneself in for being a Christian.[4] Jesus himself offered the advice that people should flee from persecution in the imminent destruction of Jerusalem (Matt 22:16). The believers fled Jerusalem during the persecution after the martyrdom of St. Stephen (Acts 8:1).

One must also understand that suffering persecution means suffering for doing good. "If you are reviled for the name of Christ, you are blessed, because the spirit of glory, which is the Spirit of God is resting on you. But let none of you suffer as a murderer, a thief, a criminal, or even as a mischief maker. Yet even if you suffer as a Christian, do not consider it a disgrace, but glorify God because you bear this name" (1 Pet 4:14–16). Early Christians were accused of many evil acts from causing disobedience to parents to cannibalism. Peter tells his readers that being accused of a terrible crime is not the same as being guilty of that crime. A Christian may be accused of something terrible, but it is better to know that God sees the suffering of the innocent. God hears the cries of Abraham's children in Egypt. God hears the cries of the unjustly accused in Tennessee (or wherever you live). We do not welcome persecution, but we may, as did Eberhard Arnold, welcome the persecutor.

Jesus told the scribes and the Pharisees that it is what comes from the heart and then out the mouths of human beings that renders them unclean. When they accused him of breaking the traditions of the elders, he did not argue the tradition of washing one's hands before they eat was wrong. Jesus argued their motivation for accusing him and his disciples came from something inside themselves that sought to find fault with other people. Matthew ends his version of the Beatitudes with a ninth one that goes with the eighth and resembles Luke's version. "Blessed are you when people revile you and persecute you and utter all kinds of evil against you falsely on my account. Rejoice and be glad for your reward is great in heaven, for in the same way they persecuted the prophets who were before you" (Matt 5:11). We must understand, too, that many times the persecutors were our own ancestors. "Woe to you scribes

4. See Middleton, "Early Christian Martyrdom."

and Pharisees, hypocrites! For you build the tombs of the prophets and decorate the graves of the righteous and you say, 'If we had lived in the days of our ancestors, we would not have taken part in shedding the blood of the prophets'" (Matt 23:29–30). Jesus argues that condemning what one's ancestors have done is not enough. We must recognize that our ancestors, for better or worse, helped in shaping us. "Thus you testify against yourselves that you are the descendants of those who murdered the prophets. Fill up, then, the measure of your ancestors" (Matt 23:31–32).

It is not an easy measure to take. I can recall some of the worst ideas about race my grandparents expressed. Do I judge them without considering how much of that way of thinking influences me? Doing that would be hypocritical on my part. Recently, I spoke with a student from Germany who appeared to fully understand what happened in the Nazi era but could not understand why it all happened. "He [Hitler] was from Austria?" None of it made sense to her. The Roman emperors who were Christian perhaps understood why their ancestors persecuted Christians in the past. They understood the affairs of state. At the same time, the average Christianized Roman would not be able to understand why their ancestors took part in the persecution. They just knew it to be wrong and that they would never do such a thing as they persecuted perceived heretics.

Persecution is not merely a fact of history—it is the reality for more people than we like to consider. We never hear about all who suffer, but sometimes those who do make excuses for their persecutors. One of the "lost boys" from South Sudan explained to me why the United States did not get involved in stopping the slaughter of his people who were Christians by the Sudanese government. "You were told," he said, "we were communists." It is easy to turn away.

Persecutors are a special type of bully. They act against weaker people to prove they can show no mercy in official circles. Just look at the example of Saul of Tarsus, the persecutor of the people of the Way before his conversion. The book of Acts tells us Paul, then called Saul, lived a life of zealous devotion to God. His zeal was so strong that he offered to persecute the blaspheming Nazarenes. He made sure the leaders of his people saw the zeal he demonstrated. Paul wanted to be noticed and known as righteous. Had his conversion never happened Paul would have likely sat on the Sanhedrin Council. Having that kind of power along with his capacity to let other people see him using it would have made him a harsh, vicious, and judgmental leader. Paul speaks of his covetousness in Rom 7. But he never tells what it was he coveted. Could it have been power, position, or reputation?

We can picture such a man arresting Christian believers while they sang, "He humbled himself and became obedient to the point of death even death on a cross" (Phil 2:8). If you were given authority to arrest people singing these words, what effect would that have on you? Answer honestly now. We can now see why Paul required such a conversion experience.

Persecutors are people with authority to carry out their actions. Their actions are often taken while being dressed up with the best motives. In the case of Saul of Tarsus, it was zeal for God, but persecutors act for other reasons, too. Finding and punishing the enemies of the people or the state is a great excuse to persecute. We may find ourselves agreeing that the leaders are defending a certain way of life and support the persecution of a minority.

Persecuting leaders look for allies to exercise mob violence. The Tulsa, Oklahoma, riots involved such actions. Lynch mobs are not headless monsters—just difficult to hold the leaders accountable.

Jesus makes it plain to the Pharisees and scribes who accuse him that motives matter more than outward gestures. Hate-filled hearts, hubris, and evil actions are not always covered by the clever use of words, appeals to authorities, or even an appeal to Scripture. He warns his followers that such people are judged not by what they say but what they do because evil within the heart is revealed by their actions. As Jesus says to his disciples, "For it is from within, from the human heart, that evil intentions come: fornication, theft murder, adultery, avarice, wickedness, deceit, licentiousness, envy, slander, pride, folly. All these evil things come from within, and they defile a person" (Mark 7:21–23).

Luke, as usual, includes a woe to accompany this Beatitude. "Woe to you when all speak well of you, for that is what their ancestors did to the false prophets" (Luke 6:26). Should we not want a good reputation as individual believers and churches? Is it not true that "a good name is better than precious ointment" (Eccl 7:1a)? Well, it is better to have a good reputation than a bad one but having approval of one's actions by evil people is not a good place to be. Jesus had a good reputation among most people for a while, yet public opinion on him wavered from time to time. Our Holy Week services, from Palm Sunday to Good Friday, make that clear.

"Just then there was in their synagogue a man with an unclean spirit, and he cried out, 'What have you to do with us Jesus of Nazareth? Have you come to destroy us? I know who you are the Holy One of God.'" Jesus could have gotten no better recommendation than from a fearful spirit from the other realm. Jesus, however, would not have it. "But Jesus rebuked him saying, 'Be silent, and come out of him!'" (Mark 1:23–25).

A similar occurrence in Philippi vexed Paul and Silas. A slave girl whose owners made a lot of money from her oracles started following them. "While she followed Paul and us, she would cry out, 'These men are slaves to the Most High God, who proclaim to you a way of salvation'" (Acts 16:17). The possessed girl follows them for a few days until Paul orders the spirit to leave the girl. Her owners become angry over losing their source of income and take him and Silas to the magistrates. Why did Paul give up such a witness from the other side?

Would you like a liar to speak about how good your character is? The devil is a liar. Demons cannot be trustworthy witnesses for the same reason. Ronald Reagan told a gathering of evangelical leaders that he knew they could not endorse him. Yet, he could endorse them. They accepted his endorsement.[5] Why should the church accept endorsements from political leaders? I know the

5. Miller, "Evangelical Presidency."

desire to have influence on the powers that be is tempting, but such powers also persecuted the prophets. We could argue we are not talking about the same people in those roles. But as we saw with Kings Saul, David, and Solomon, the people in positions of authority are fallible human beings facing the temptations of power. Those who try to influence them are just as fallible and tempted.

The text quoted earlier from Peter helps us understand the importance of the good name of Christ. We are honored to suffer in his name if that is the true reason we suffer. Paul and Silas find themselves before the magistrates in Philippi accused of subverting Roman law. Their accusers own a slave that is no longer useful to them. It is about money. But loss of income from exploiting the suffering of the girl will not impress the magistrates. Paul and Silas are accused of something else instead. "These men are disturbing our city; they are Jews and are advocating customs that are not lawful for us as Romans to adopt or observe" (Acts 16:20b–21). The good citizens of Philippi join in the attack. Why? They do not care about a slave girl or lost income. They feel their sense of identity is being attacked by foreign influence. We are Romans! In Ephesus the chant will be "Great is Artemis of the Ephesians" (Acts 19:28b). Mobs are stirred up into persecuting a smaller group because they are made to feel threatened. Peter says we should not suffer as murderers, thieves, criminals, or mischief makers. In other words, we should not live as though we are a threat to anyone.

ENDURING PERSECUTION

How long should we put up with persecution? Persecution comes in different levels. One can suffer persecution from specialized tax burdens, ghettoization, forbidding trade or relief given, beating, pogroms, jailing, and death. The less extreme the levels of persecution, the more sustainable they tend to be. The more extreme levels are more likely to be unsustainable. The emotional outrage that goes into pogroms, beatings, rioting, and lynching do not last for very long, but if persecution is the rule, the likelihood of such things happening increases. So, the question of how long it should be tolerated remains.

Endurance is a value that Paul says produces character that leads to hope. "And not only that, we also boast in our sufferings, knowing that suffering produces endurance, and endurance produces character, and character produces hope, and hope does not disappoint us, because God's love has been poured into our hearts through the Holy Spirit that has been given to us" (Rom 5:3–5). Christian endurance is needed to withstand temptation from boredom, despair, or persecution. Like most people, I wonder how much I could endure if I had to and at the same time hope I never have to find out.

Athletes challenge their physical endurance as a matter of course. In their case, the suffering produces enough endurance to continue suffering until the end of the contest. If they win the competition they receive honors. If they lose after having done their best, they still receive my respect for doing something I cannot do.

Having listened to some stories people tell about suffering and surviving severe child abuse, I am often convinced I could not have survived their story. I respect them for overcoming and seeking healing. However, there are many other people who are so broken by their experience that they cannot find a way to deal with the conflicting emotions, especially the justifiable rage they felt toward everyone who might have rescued them.

The actor Andrew Garfield stars in two major films dealing with issues related to faith and persecution. He plays the role of Desmond Doss in *Hacksaw Ridge*, about a conscientious objector who served as a medic in a major battle against the Japanese in World War II.[6] This biopic details his rejection of violence as a young man who is persecuted by his fellow soldiers and the officers of the army. He later saves many of the lives of wounded soldiers by remaining to help them after the attack was abandoned. Doss the coward becomes Doss the hero and is awarded the Congressional Medal of Honor. The movie ends with the triumph of endurance, faith, and courage.

6. Gibson, *Hacksaw Ridge*.

The other film is *Silence*.[7] It is not a film in which one sees the triumph of endurance, faith, and courage. The film is a remake from an earlier 1971 Japanese film about some of the first Jesuit missionaries to Japan, both based on a novel by Shusaku Endo. Early Japanese Christians suffered a lot of persecution for believing in a foreign deity and bringing in ways of living that were alien to Japanese imperial values. It sounds like a familiar story, but Father Sebastião Rodrigues, played by Garfield, gives up his faith under severe torture. He is portrayed as a broken human who cannot escape the void left because he could not endure. The fear he continues to feel comes across very well.

"But we are not among those who shrink back and so are lost, but among those who have faith and so are saved" (Heb 10:39). The writer of Hebrews appears very harsh toward people who break under persecution. Apparently fighting fear in people by instilling a greater fear in them was used among early believers. "Do not fear those who kill the body but not the soul; rather fear him who can destroy both body and soul in hell" (Matt 10:28). The doubt and fear of the apostate priest in *Silence* is based in his suffering. Did he ever truly believe? Was he so filled with doubt that he broke rather than endure to the end? How do faithful people overcome fear in the face of persecution?

Paul offers this gentle advice. "I consider that the present sufferings of this present time are not worth comparing with the glory about to be revealed to us" (Rom 8:18). He further argues that we do not suffer alone, but that the whole of creation suffers as we do and waits with us for our final redemption. He does not say that suffering is itself redemptive. God is not testing our character, endurance, or faith. Our hope is not being tested either. If anything is being tested it is God's grace and love. When we suffer, we ask where God is. Does God truly love me? Where Jesus tells us it would be better to fear the one who can destroy everything about us, he continues, "Are not two sparrows sold for a penny? Yet not one of them will fall to the ground apart from your Father. And even the very hairs of your head are all counted. So do

7. Scorsese, *Silence*.

not be afraid; you are of more value than many sparrows" (Matt 10:29–31).

We look around us at the suffering of the creation and remember that God knows what is happening with all of it. My perspective allows me to see a dead finch near the bird feeder. It did not just appear there when I walked outside and looked. It had been there for some time after whatever killed it. I did not see it die because reality is not subject to my perspective. If another bird flies overhead while I am looking at the dead bird on the ground, it does not mean the one over me is unreal in some way. Someone else may be looking at the bird and not see me because that person cannot see over the fence. Jesus says there is one whose perspective sees everything as it happens. Hagar, the misused servant of Abraham and Sarah, declared God sees all of us (Gen 16:13). God saw her and not just Abraham.

The writer of Hebrews continues with the great cloud of witnesses who lived in faith before God. The faithful people presented by the writer did not endure because they were sinlessly perfect people. They are considered saints because of their faith and hope in their God. The writer compares them to the Christian readers of his letter, "They confessed that they were strangers and foreigners on the earth for people who speak this way make it clear that they are seeking a homeland." Earlier Abraham, Isaac, and Jacob are described in their lives as looking "forward to the city that has foundations, whose builder and architect is God" (Heb 11:10).

The stories of the victorious saints are important morale boosters for what Christians may be asked to endure. However, it is good for us to know about those who failed in their faithfulness so that we know the door to return is always open. Christians in comfortable situations must remember that grace and love are to prevail through all times whether those times are good or evil.

I have not answered the question of how long Christians should endure persecution because the New Testament writers, at least the earliest ones, assumed the final redemption, the *parousia*, or revelation was to happen in their generation. Scholars speak of the *delayed parousia* when they talk about some of the comments in later letters. "First of all you must understand this, that in the last days scoffers will come . . . and saying, 'Where is the promise of his coming? For ever since our ancestors died, all things continue as they were from the day of creation!'" (2 Pet 3:3–4). The letter continues with descriptions of the last day and how God has interrupted history. It also says time is meaningless to God. No timetable has been set for Jesus' return. "Therefore, beloved, while you are waiting for these things, strive to be found by him at peace, without spot or blemish; and regard the patience of the Lord as salvation" (2 Pet 3:14–15a). It is a short letter that is more like a sermon reminding the believers that bad actions were taken against the faithful of the past, but that does not mean the faithful should fall into doing the same things themselves.

The second letter to the Thessalonians is another one that deals with this issue of the delayed revelation. "As to the coming of our Lord Jesus Christ and our being gathered together to him, we beg you, brothers and sisters, not to be quickly shaken in mind or alarmed, either by spirit or by letter, as though from us, to the effect that the day of the Lord is already here" (2 Thess 2:1–2). Why later letters were needed is obvious. People were losing hope. Were they fools for ever believing the gospel story? "For this purpose he called you through our proclamation of the good news, so that you may obtain the glory of our Lord Jesus Christ. So then, brothers and sisters, stand firm and hold fast to the traditions that you were taught by us, either by word of mouth or by our letter" (2 Thess 2:14–15).

People will also lose hope because of the anger of having suffered too much. John the Revelator gives us insight into this in his Apocalypse, or as we name it, Revelation. John is given messages to the seven churches, and then describes his vision of heaven that he received while living in exile on the island of Patmos. The great visions of God on a throne surrounded by creatures proclaiming praise and the Lamb who is worthy to open the seals are stopped by an outcry. "When he opened the fifth seal, I saw under the altar the souls of those who had been slaughtered for the word of God and the testimony they had given; they cried out with a loud voice, 'Sovereign lord, holy and true, how long will it be before you judge and avenge our blood on the inhabitants of the earth?'" (Rev 6:9–10).

The seven churches that are addressed in this book have their own situations and temptations, and some are persecuted. They are all either undergoing or about to undergo a process of painful purification. The churches of Ephesus, Thyatira, and Philadelphia are described as having "patient endurance." They are about to have their patience and endurance tested by what is to happen soon.

The martyrs who were slaughtered for the testimony of Christ are given white robes and told to . . . rest a little while longer. More martyrs are to be made and will be added to their number. It is interesting that they are not told to wait or patiently endure a little while longer. They are told to rest.

People in heaven wanting revenge presents its own conundrums for Christians who do not suffer persecution, but the point is simple. Patience runs out eventually, while endurance breaks down. One wonders why the attempts to answer these concerns become confusing. The fact that there is no final answer to persecution is why Jesus declares the persecuted blessed.

People do not choose to be persecuted. Faithfulness to our beliefs and who we are is a matter of personal integrity. The integrity of the community depends on the faithfulness of individual members. Plato and Aristotle understood the need for community integrity. Yet, they differed on which came first. One Hebrew writer knew the importance of group integrity for the sake of its members. While telling the story of dedicating the temple, the writer describes a second vision from God to King Solomon, who is told concerning the temple, "if my people who are called by my name humble themselves, pray, seek my face, and turn from their wicked ways, then I will hear from heaven, and will forgive their sin and heal their land" (2 Chr 7:14). Many people use this text as an email signature line or a social media meme. Without the context though, we misunderstand how disasters, even naturally occurring ones, can bring about social conflict. The personal faithfulness of Solomon helps the faithfulness of his people.

Jeremiah does not consider the faithfulness of the king or the people as the source of healing the land. God will bring about the restoration of the land. "See, I am going to gather them from all the lands to which I drove them . . . I will bring them back to this place and I will settle them in safety. They shall be my people, and I will be their God" (Jer 32:37–38). God is the source of faithfulness and healing the people.

Christians who suffer persecution in isolation from other believers are more likely to lose hope than if they suffer together. If the community maintains its integrity, the individual will have an easier time doing so. The advantage of community is the main reason Paul gives for church discipline not to be too harsh. When the church in Corinth set an offender outside of the fellowship of the community, Paul instructed the punishment was enough, and the offender should be forgiven. "So I urge you to reaffirm your love for him and console him . . . and we do this so that we may not be outwitted by Satan; for we are not ignorant of his designs" (2 Cor 8–11). Earlier in the first letter Paul, wrote about the community tolerating a person living in an incestuous relationship who should be removed from the congregation, but he now counsels that such actions should leave the door of repentance open.

These examples give us insight into how long we should endure persecution. The persecuted are not recognized by the persecutors as children of God. However, persecuted Christians must recognize the persecutors as beloved by God. A time will come when the persecution will end. The slaughtered martyrs of Revelation are instructed to rest until the set numbers of their brothers and sisters come to be among them. When the persecution ends, Christians will be faced with choices of response. Our response should be to do whatever heals.

PERSECUTION WITHIN THE CHURCH

Persecution comes from the church to some of its members. It is a shame, but even Paul had his critics. Yet sometimes the persecution is used to protect the church by covering up instances of sexual abuse. When the clergy abuse of children scandal broke it was discovered that some of the families of the victims were threatened by church leaders and their lawyers.

Many people have explained, sometimes in detail, how they have been harmed by the church. Religious abuse does occur. Many of these people find it easier to manage their pain by leaving the church altogether. Some have remained within the church even though they have gone to another congregation that helped them through their pain.

There are other people who claim the church persecuted them just because they did not get their own way about something. What often happens in these cases is that the argument between them and someone else in the matter became toxic enough to feel like they were being persecuted. Church disputes should never be allowed to go so far, but they often do. Why does this happen?

The ways of the world infect the thinking of church leaders, both clergy and lay people. In this present time, we think of the church in terms of businesses. We purchase liability insurance, invest certain funds, and have finance campaigns. It is understandable that many leaders approach church business as, well, business. We should ask ourselves what is more important, the capital fundraising campaign or our brother or sister across the table who honestly disagrees about how we spend the money when we get it?

Resentments over such arguments will build against someone with whom we sing "And They Will Know We Are Christians" on Sunday morning. This is simply not the way of Jesus. Being resentful then leads us into intolerable situations, including many evils like that of being persecutors. It is better to recognize our sin before we become people who hate our brothers based on our bad feelings.

Paul says we should not leave room for the hatred that is opposed to the way of Christ. James counsels, "You must understand this, my beloved; let everyone be quick to listen, slow to speak, slow to anger; for your anger does not produce God's righteousness. Therefore rid yourselves of all sordidness and rank growth of wickedness, and welcome with meekness the implanted word that has the power to save your souls" (Jas 1:19–20). We considered this text in an earlier chapter, but it applies to what Paul says in 2 Corinthians. We do not wish to become people who are harsh with our neighbors and accusatory to God as the martyrs in Revelation appear to be. We wish to be pure in heart and merciful peacemakers.

THE GIFT OF THE NEIGHBOR

A famous story of martyrdom during the Reformation is that of the Anabaptist Dirk Willems.[8] In the early winter of 1569, a guard pursued Willems after he escaped imprisonment in Asperen in Holland. Willems crossed over an ice-covered pond. The guard, on the other hand, broke through the ice and yelled for help. Willems had a choice. He could continue running, leaving the persecutor to die. He chose instead to go back and help the guard. After rescuing the guard, Willems was arrested and brought back to Asperen. The story goes that the guard wished to free Willems. His superiors would not allow it. Willems died a martyr's death.

Here we may recall the saying that "No good deed goes unpunished." Willems apparently believed he would be indirectly responsible for the guard's death by not helping him. Perhaps, he looked at the situation in another way, but we can safely say Willems understood the value of the neighbor.

We often hear the proverb "Good fences make good neighbors." When a farmer owns animals that might eat his neighbor's crops, good fences are a necessity to keeping peace. In suburbia, it may mean keep your dog in your yard and out of mine. It could also be taken to mean "You mind your business, and I will mind mine." Even when we consider these thoughts, we should remember the neighbor is a gift.

Many people find it easier to deal with people like themselves, but in a pluralistic society, our neighbors may have life experiences very different from our own. Your neighbor may seem loud and obnoxious, while your neighbor may think you are too quiet and

---

8. *Mennonite Quarterly Review*, "Compassion for the Enemy."

withdrawn. Christians are required to love our neighbors and find some way to not only coexist but build a community.

Living in parsonages, I have been the outsider who comes to the neighborhood. People who have known each other for a long time suddenly have this new family as their new neighbors. What would they be like? One community my family and I were moving to had people standing in their yards hoping to catch a glimpse of the new clergy family. I was sure to wave. It was amusing when people would say with evident relief, "I am glad you are so normal." I wonder what they feared when the Annual Conference sent them new neighbors.

Should the new person in the community be made to feel welcome? Yes. Unfortunately, it often becomes the responsibility of the new people to demonstrate that they want to become part of the community. The newcomer reaches out to the new community to show that the neighbor is beloved by God. This action goes back to the principle expressed by Paul that we are to live in peace with everyone if we can.

We live in a time when people think Jesus got it all wrong. Pastors are worried that too many of their church members think Jesus should have allowed "Love your neighbors but hate your enemies" to stand without any correction. Some congregants have said to their pastors, we cannot love our enemies, they must be crushed. A recent letter to the editor to my local newspaper had one writer claim members of another political party should be destroyed. Something is wrong here.

When I told my father I was writing a book on the Beatitudes, he said, "All churches would be better off if we concentrated on following the Beatitudes." As this book makes clear though, that is easier to say than do. The story of Eulpus implies that it may be easier to die for Jesus than to live for Christ. When discussing divorce and remarriage with Jesus, his disciples reply, "If such is the case of a man with his wife, it is better not to marry." Jesus explained that is easier said than done. "Not everyone can accept this teaching, but only those to whom it is given . . . there are eunuchs who have made themselves eunuchs for the sake of the kingdom of heaven. Let anyone accept this who can" (Matt 19:10b–12). It is easier to live the way of Christ if we want to live. Few of us can ever die the death of martyrs without hating our persecutors. It is better to live and be perfected in love.

Bibliography

Ateek, Naim Stifan. *Justice and Only Justice: A Palestinian Theology of Liberation.* Maryknoll, NY: Orbis, 1989.

Brady, D. Kohler, and H. U. Zheng. "Novel Estimates of Mortality Associated with Poverty in the U.S." *Journal of the American Medical Association Internal Medicine* 183.6 (2023) 618–19.

Chesterton, G. K. *The Life of Saint Francis of Assisi.* N.p.: OK Publishing, 2019. E-book.

Crowe, Cameron, dir. *We Bought a Zoo.* Screenplay by Alin Brosh McKenna and Cameron Crowe. 20th Century Fox, 2011. DVD.

"Debasing Dissent." *New York Times*, Nov. 16, 1967, 46.

"Eberhard Arnold's Life and Work." Eberhard Arnold: Founder of the Bruderhof, n.d. www.eberhardarnold.com/biography.

Eller, Vernard. *Christian Anarchy: Jesus' Primacy Over the Powers.* Eugene, OR: Wipf & Stock, 1999.

Gibson, Mel, dir. *Hacksaw Ridge.* Screenplay by Andrew Knight and Robert Schenkkan. Summit Entertainment et al., Australia, 2016.

Holocaust Encyclopedia. "Abba Kovner." United States Holocaust Memorial Museum, n.d. https://encyclopedia.ushmm.org/content/en/article/abba-kovner.

Job, Reuben Philip. *Three Simple Rules: A Wesleyan Way of Living.* Nashville: Abingdon, 2010.

JPS Tanakh. Philadelphia: Jewish Publication Society, 1985.

Lewis, C. S. *The Problem of Pain.* New York: Macmillan, 1962.

———. *That Hideous Strength.* New York: Collier, 1965.

McCullough, David. *John Adams.* New York: Simon and Schuster, 2001.

McDoom, Omar Shahabudin. "Contested Counting: Toward a Rigorous Estimate of the Death Toll in Rwanda." June 2019. https://eprints.lse.ac.uk/103205/1/McDoom_Contested_Counting_accepted_version.pdf

Mennonite Quarterly Review. "Compassion for the Enemy." N.d. https://www.goshen.edu/mqr/dirk-willems/.

Middleton, Paul. "Early Christian Martyrdom: A Statement for the Defense." *Journal of Theological Studies* 64.2 (2013) 556–73.

Miller, Steven P. "The Evangelical Presidency: Ronald Reagan's Dangerous Love Affair with the Christian Right." *Salon*, May 18, 2014. https://www.salon.

com/2014/05/18/the_evangelical_presidency_reagans_dangerous_love_
affair_with_the_christian_right/.

Isaac, Munther. "'Christ in the Rubble': Palestinian Pastor Delivers Powerful
Christmas Sermon from Bethlehem." YouTube video, 2023. https://www.
youtube.com/watch?v=Md_hw_A-oIs.

Rakin, Alan, dir. "The Battle of Mayberry." *The Andy Griffith Show*, season 6,
episode 29. Aired April 4, 1966. Paramount+ streaming.

Rule of St. Benedict. Translated by Leonard Doyle, St. John's Abbey. Collegeville,
MN: Liturgical, 1948.

Scorsese, Martin, dir. *Silence.* Screenplay by Jay Cocks and Martin Scorsese.
SharpSword Films et al., Taiwan, 2016.

Shakespeare, William. *The Merchant of Venice.* Great Books of the Western
World 24. Chicago: Encyclopedia Britannica, 1990.

———. *The Life of King Henry V.* Great Books of the Western World 24.
Chicago: Encyclopedia Britannica, 1990.

Sheshadri, Raja. "Pygmies in the Congo Basin and Conflict." *ICE Case Studies*
163 (Dec. 2005).

Simonetti, Manlio, et al., eds. *Ancient Christian Commentary on the Scriptures:
New Testament.* Vol. 1, *Matthew 1–13.* Lisle, IL: IVP Academic, 2001.

Tolstoy, Leo. *Walk in the Light and Twenty-Three Tales.* Translated by Leo
Wiener and Louise and Aylmer Maude. N.p.: Digireads, 2020.

Tutu, Desmond Mpilo. *No Future Without Forgiveness.* New York: Image, 2000.

Yad Vashem. "Borkowska, Anna." N.d. https://collections.yadvashem.org/en/
righteous/4014050.